HIGH-PERFORMANCE DRIVING

How to Use the Techniques
of the World's Great Racing Drivers
for Better, Faster, Safer Driving

PAUL PETERSEN

illustrated by F. MICHAEL MORRIS

photographs by BARRY TENIN

SIMON AND SCHUSTER • NEW YORK

SBN 671-27117-2
Library of Congress Catalog Card Number: 73-15487
Designed by Edith Fowler
Manufactured in the United States of America

1   2   3   4   5   6   7   8   9   10

ACKNOWLEDGMENTS

F. Michael Morris, for his expertise and friendship and his art.

Barry Tenin, for his aid and his camera.

Goodyear Tire and Rubber Company, especially Dave Harrison, Publicity; Robert W. Yeager, Group Leader, Tire Design Research; and Jack E. Brown, Tire Design Research.

Tony Sherman, for taking time to teach and understand.

For DAVID . . .
    the value of life
    is knowing
    that no man can imagine
    without it.
    It's the same with a friend.

CONTENTS

PREFACE

A yawning chasm separates the world of the professional racer and the average motorist yet both are inextricably bound to the limits of automobiles.

Racing uncontestably stretches the capabilities of cars as each technological innovation produces machines that go better, stop faster, and corner more quickly. These advances are finding their way into the cars currently available to the general public. Unfortunately, the skills necessary to make use of, or even control, these new levels of performance have not sifted down to the people who need them most.

During the past twenty years, speeds and capabilities have risen at a much faster rate than anyone would have dared dream when motor racing regained its footing after the war years. For all its advances, the automobile is still controlled by little-changed man. The sad reality is that cars are sounder than the people who drive them. Whether this is because cars are so endemic to the environment, like light bulbs, that no one cares about the whys, or because people just don't have the time to truly appreciate the function of an automobile, no one can say.

Some would say it's better to have cars overdesigned. When you consider, however, the misuse of automobiles that happens at any hour of the clock, or any flip of the calendar, you must take pause to wonder about the efficacy of that thought. A car bears little of the blame for the situations it finds itself in.

Driver training and licensing programs offer little to the general public in ways and means of controlling that 4,000-pound missile and even less in terms of the reasons for a car's behavior.

This book attempts to fill the gap between garage and paddock in terms the layman can understand. It is not meant as a racing manual. Others, far more qualified than myself, have presented literature aimed toward the man who wants to race. This book is for the man on the street, with all its ramifications.

As an enthusiast who has enjoyed a better-than-average opportunity to try my hand at "life at speed," I found a curious lack of a comprehensive outline written for the average motorist; and never satisfied when I didn't know, I undertook a voyage of discovery that led to answers, to be sure, but answers intelligible only if one had a master's in engineering or a sensory background that already included some time "on the edge." There are millions of cars on the road, and most of them are driven by people who couldn't care less about anything other than getting from here to there. But what about the driver who is just starting his lifelong love of cars? Where does he go for information? How can he safely set out in a car that is capable of so much more than he?

Driving at speed is, in the last analysis, a matter for the senses. But when those senses are rooted in fundamental knowledge, the possibilities for error are reduced. If this book does nothing but lead the reader toward even higher levels of understanding the safe and responsible use of a car, then it has served its purpose.

INTRODUCTION
THE BIRTH OF AN OBSESSION

Cobra, "born in grace and defiled by Ford," or so the saying went. I bought her at eighteen and considered myself the luckiest man on earth. I will never forget the first time I settled into her ironing-board seat. The hinged brake and clutch pedal and heavily sprung throttle strained for my command. Her roll bar surrounded me like a huge staple. She had a stubby gearshift lever that promised short, precise throws from gear to gear. Two thousands pounds on an English chassis and a 289-cubic-inch heart that delivered 300 horses. Outside silver, inside black. She was a four-wheel beast that stirred the heart and bewitched the soul.

I met her on the seventeenth of May, 1963, and for two weeks we got acquainted, my Cobra and I. It was a Mexican courtship filled with innuendoes of things to come and strict adherence to all known conventions. I collected three speeding tickets that first night.

On the third Friday it was back to the shop for new tires. The stock issue lasted 1900 miles. Her new paws were Goodyear, those big fat Bluestreaks. I also picked up a helmet, had brake scoops installed, acquired stiffer shocks, and got a tune all because I had signed up for Carroll Shelby's School of High-Performance Driving at Riverside Raceway.

The following Monday morning I was in the Ramada Inn coffee shop in Riverside, ten minutes early for a seven o'clock meeting with John Timanus, who was to be my instructor. When he walked in, I couldn't help but note that his left arm was in a cast. He had broken it a few days earlier, he explained, when he had ducked under a fence in his Lotus. It is a sobering sight to see your high-performance driving instructor crippled because of a racing accident. John was an angular fellow with the demeanor of an engineer, except when he talked about cars.

There were three "students." One, a doctor, had what I—the proud new owner of a Cobra—referred to as a plastic bathtub (Corvette). It was new and race-prepared. The other trainee had trailered his Lotus Seven a long way, bringing with him a friend who served as gopher and wrench (a "go-for" and mechanic). I completed the trio with my factory stock Cobra.

Timanus wasted little time and in short order we were at the track, fidgeting in the dusty infield of Turn Nine, scene of some of the scariest, most spectacular, and sadly fatal accidents in racing. Turn Nine is a sweeping right-hander that can be taken past 90 mph. It has a sharply banked profile and a sinister white wall all along the outside to keep an errant driver from spilling over the edge and crashing into the bleak desert below.

With blackboard and chalk, John drew an outline of the turn and ran through such concerns as apexes, footprints, exit speeds, and other technical matters that didn't mean much to me. I was anxious to get on the track and show up Stirling Moss.

The Lotus fellow went first. A Lotus Seven moving through a 90-mile-an-hour turn is not the most thrilling sight in the world. In fact, it's downright boring. There's just no fuss in a Lotus. The dude got in and cruised out to the track, following the "line" as drawn on John's blackboard. He came into the turn at speed, no sliding, no loose fanny, no noise. He just buzzed around the turn. John had placed an orange pylon on the inside of the turn to mark the apex and the Lotus driver hit it time after time, steadily increasing his speed. John, stopwatch in hand, timed him from entrance to exit until he was satisfied, then waved him in.

I could hardly contain myself, but John had read me correctly. He knew my impatience could be fatal. Owning a Cobra meant squat out there. So, I waited.

The doctor was next. He hustled the bulky 'Vette out there like a pro, the car sounding lean and mean, as the Lotus crew and I settled down to watch while John took up his position near the pylon, stop-watch in hand.

Following John's instructions to the letter, the doctor took it easy for two circuits and then gradually increased his speed. On his fourth pass he was up to 70.

On his fifth encounter with Turn Nine, the doctor got in over his head. He came off the straight well below the Corvette's ability to negotiate the turn but above his own capabilities. He had the wrong line, and in trying to haul the car back into position, he managed to swing it sideways. Fear and ignorance kept his foot on the throttle, and he started up the banking toward the white wall. He frantically tried to assert his control but only succeeded in making matters worse. He steered into the spin, catching his upward flight, but his right foot still bore down on the loud pedal. He began to dive toward the inside of the turn, headed directly at John, who stood his ground. The whipping 'Vette slid off the track and into the infield, narrowly missing John, and there it expired. Why it didn't flip I'll never know. The doctor had come off the asphalt sideways, crimping the pylon beneath the undercarriage. We ran over to the car as the doctor climbed out.

John, the calmest among us, addressed the quaking doctor. "You came in too low and got on it much too early."

I finally began to listen.

The Corvette had sustained no damage but the doctor made quite a show of walking around inspecting everything. He finally announced he was going to have the car checked, "just to make sure it's all right." He drove off and never came back.

Because my Cobra and the Corvette had similar handling and power characteristics, I listened intently as John explained what I had just witnessed. The key word was "respect"; and when my turn came, John's comments and cautions were firmly planted in my mind. With shaking knees and a heartbeat that rivaled my engine speed, I crept around Turn Nine for the first time.

My senses, alert and active, transmitted all kinds of data to my brain. The track was wide and smooth, bent sharply where the straight met the turn's banking. I noted the slight ripple at the mid-point of the turn, back some 50 feet from the apex John had marked for me.

My next trip around Turn Nine was slightly faster, and the whole exercise began to be an experience—the mating of man and machine into a single, cohesive whole. On my third trip I used third gear, low for the speed but in line with my orders. At 70, centrifugal force tried to pull me up the banking, and the tires, particularly up front, began to protest. Out of the corner of my eye I saw John smile as I passed the pylon for the third time. I knew, even though the speed was low, I had hit the correct line.

I started to cook on the fourth circuit, getting my speed up to a point where I had to brake before entering the turn. The Cobra's personality began to change on that lap, and, as a result, mine did too. I could feel every movement, every revolution, every force as the car did its thing. I was right on the "line."

The fifth trip brought matters to a head. In this training session we used the quarter-mile cutoff shortly after the exit from Turn Nine, which dumped out on the back straight. I was able to get my speed up to 120 mph before I got to Turn Nine, which meant I had to brake and downshift. I stabbed at the binders, "heel and toe," as I shifted from fourth to third and eased the Cobra onto the line. The hard, steady right would direct me down to the apex if I judged the drift properly. It felt right so I began to tease the throttle and the Cobra caught its balance. My path was correct and I was on full throttle when I brushed the apex. The car rippled under me with all that power being fed to the wheels. Coming out of the turn, my arc widened naturally without turning the steering wheel and took me out to within three feet of the outside guardrail.

That exit from Turn Nine was one of the supreme moments of my life. The execution had been good, really good; and I knew that I could do it again and again. I proved it to myself on the next circuit and the one after that. Exhilaration squeezed my chest as I steadily increased the speed and precision. Time vanished until John waved me in.

I tracked through the infield dirt as John, his face mirroring his approval, and the Lotus guys walked over to me. I killed the engine and just sat there as the Cobra breathed out her fire, groaning and popping in mock complaint to the abuse she had been built for.

"Aren't you getting out?" someone asked.

"No. Not ever," I said.

It was a voice I didn't know. It reflected a sense of awe, of purpose, and even of humility that I had never felt before. Sitting in that hot cockpit, Castrol Forty fumes all about me, the experience slipped into memory, but not without leaving its mark. A total experience had filled a space I didn't know existed, and with its passing I felt empty.

"You'll do it again, Paul," John said gently.

But not for the first time, I thought.

1
DRIVER ATTITUDE

The object of this book is control—control over yourself, your automobile, the situation, and, most of all, your attitude. Other passengers, alcohol, and drugs are just a few of the things that can destroy your ability to control a car at speed. An automobile is the single most lethal item in our environment. It kills indiscriminately. It can break up a family or wipe it out. The sad part is that a car doesn't have to be a weapon. If you are serious about driving at speed, turn to the Appendix and make a note of the schools of high-performance driving scattered around the country. They are the places to do it.

Control is not turned on and off. It should be with you from the moment you buckle up and back out the driveway. As you settle in your car, take a moment to think about the purpose of your forthcoming drive. If you think this book will help you get home from the office five minutes earlier, you're reading the wrong book.

Speed for speed's sake should be left in the hands of men who make their living at it. They don't arrive at their level of skill without practice, disappointments, and most likely some close brushes with "the big cash out." Don't fool yourself into thinking you are Emerson Fittipaldi because you once controlled a skid that was the result of an error you committed in the first place.

On our roadways, situations occur with surprising regularity that require knowledge and use of the fundamentals of high-performance driving in order to survive. These techniques are what I hope to share with you. If on some dark night, you manage to escape destruction by what you learn from this book, then your money and my time have been well spent.

With all the broad, well-lighted and smoothly paved roads in America and with cars to match, we Americans have forgotten how to drive. With the slightest trace of rain, folks start sliding all over the place. Our freeways all bear traces of some character's latest panic stop. You can't drive two miles without seeing the marks of an accident along highway dividers. In almost every case, the driver, not the car, couldn't cope with the hazard.

I'll have to make certain assumptions about my readers. First, you are not wholly ignorant about the various components of a car. Second, you are not foolish enough to attempt what will be outlined in succeeding pages in a car ill-suited to the task. A car with bad brakes, poor shocks, bald tires, or one with passengers has all the possibilities of tragedy. Third, you are sensible enough to find a parking lot, an unused road, or other such safe spot to practice. Again, the best place to start is a race track under the proper supervision. An abandoned airfield or an empty, smooth field also makes a fine practice pad. You need a spot with no surprises. Fourth, you are trying to please no one but yourself. Understand that the gratification which comes with achieving your goal is personal and need not involve anyone else.

Bear in mind that this is not a text for racing, even though most of the methods discussed would apply directly to motoring around a race course. Also keep in mind that the goal is to help you focus all your skills and knowledge, from braking to shifting, from cornering to acceleration, into a pattern that will serve you anywhere, in any car, and under all conditions. While aspects of driving at speed will be discussed in individual sections, the object is to create an integrated, cohesive environment where knowledge, habit, and good driving sense are wholly joined.

A car is a machine and thus something that conforms to set standards and physical laws that are not beyond comprehension. When driven within those boundaries, it will respond beautifully and give the driver an extraordinary amount of satisfaction. If it were a question of go, stop, turn, and nothing else, this would be a shorter book. The technical aspects may seem tedious but they must be mastered to bring about the proper attitude.

Any car, whether a fire-breathing Group Seven monster or a Volkswagen, is an inert collection of bits and pieces without the driver to activate the components. Driving requires concentration and co-ordination between man and machine. There are five parts to driving and four of them, brain, eyes, hands, and feet, relate to the driver. The fifth is, of course, the car. We will begin with the major problem, the driver.

2
DOES IT FIT?

Despite the presence of adjustments in seat location, back-rest rake, and steering wheel, drivers consistently place themselves in positions that will not allow them to use all of their controls positively. A poor seating position does more than any amount of time behind the wheel to create driver fatigue and its attendant dangers.

The most common fault is getting too close to the steering wheel. There is no need for this situation in today's automobiles where the controls work quite easily. When you sit too close, your arms are bent awkwardly and any movement of the wheel past the 180-degree mark finds your elbows either high in the air or in contact with the side door.

If you are too close, you also run afoul of the bottom of the wheel when you move your feet from throttle to brake or actuate the clutch. Your thighs should not be lifted to work the pedals. Pedal pressures and steering effort have been reduced in modern cars and it is not necessary to be "on top of things."

On the other hand, you don't want to have the seat so far back that the distance to the pedals is too far and the reach to the farthest gear (usually third) requires you to lean forward. That creates tension through the upper back and shoulders. There is always a middle ground. Things should fall "easily to hand," as the saying goes.

All seating adjustments should be carried out with the belts done up snugly. Seat belts locate you securely, and the support of lap and shoulder belts reduces driver fatigue.

The reach to the gear farthest away from you should be at the extreme of your reach. The proper seating position should permit placing your hands at the three and nine o'clock settings on the steering wheel with a slight bend at the elbows. Most of the cars adaptable to high-performance driving have excellent controls and an almost infinite variety of seat adjustments to facilitate custom fitting. A new car or a strange car always requires that little extra time to find, figure out, and use the different positions available. Find a position that gives the most thigh, side, and lower-back support, and remember that seat belts and shoulder harness add to the feeling of solidarity and sense of oneness with the machine.

The lap belt should be fitted snugly across the large bones of the hip. They are built to withstand impact and compression. The shoulder harness should be snug; and with the diagonal restraint systems, care should be taken to make sure the belt is not twisted or run on a line too close to the neck. A belt edge can be as sharp as a knife's. Professional drivers use the over-the-shoulder or doubled shoulder harness to avoid this hazard.

Familiarity breeds control, not contempt, in the case of an automobile. Make sure you are familiar with your car by giving yourself this simple test. Sit in your car with eyes closed and name all your gauges and switches left to right and actuate every control as you name it, and the warning lights, too. With eyes still closed, picture every edge of your car. Where is the right rear corner? Do you feel comfortable in your car with your eyes closed? Most people don't. You should be able to reach and use all of your controls by feel.

Almost all the information we receive while driving comes through our eyes. The way we see and what we see through are extremely important. Clean glasses and windshield are crucial. A slanting late-afternoon sun on a dirty windshield has killed more than one hapless pilot. Properly adjusted and clean mirrors are also essential, not just to pick up the sight of a police cruiser, but to locate yourself and your car to your surroundings. For night driving, leave a small dark spot in the mirror placement so you can avoid the glare of trailing headlights by shifting right or left. Don't rely on this completely, however.

Two other systems mean better sight: headlights and the windshield washer/wipers. The headlights should have clean lenses, and replace the blades of your wipers if they leave streaks or, worse, make tiny scratches on the glass. A working washer system with the proper additive is also very helpful. A soft clean cloth under the seat and a can of spray-type window cleaner in the glove compartment may also come in handy.

Instruments, necessary as they are, take your eyes off the road. Locating the gauges—tachometer, oil pressure, water temperature—just off your normal line of vision through the windshield makes checking the health of your engine an easy matter. Reading gauges is made even easier if the faces of the instruments are rotated so that when things are normal all the pointers are vertical. Changes are more readily seen.

The tachometer is the most important dial and this too should be rotated so the most important marking on its face, the red line, is at the top. The red line indicates the upper limit on engine revs.

The ability to pick up movement is an integral part of driving; any object hanging from a rear-view mirror, anything at all, reduces your peripheral sense. You may not see that car from the corner of your eye because your mind is accustomed to seeing movement there.

Matches, cigarettes, glasses, and other such essential nonsense should be put away in the glove compartment. Their movement on the dash takes away your concentration. That beanbag ashtray may catch ashes, but it can also slide off and get under the pedals, a potentially dangerous condition.

The ability to "place" a car, knowing *exactly* the location of all four wheels, the corners, and ends, involves depth perception. You should be able to pull within three inches of any obstacle in front, within six inches at the rear, and within six inches on either side. That's something you can practice just pulling into the garage. Later in this book, you will be asked to place your car on a line that will be very close to the verge of the road and you should know where the edges are.

As suggested earlier, hands should be on the wheel just above the three and nine o'clock positions. Don't clutch at the wheel. A death grip on the steering wheel creates tension and induces driver fatigue. Gloves can be a great aid if you're driving off-road machinery or expect to be working hard at the wheel for an appreciable length of time. Mittens or any other type of hand covering destroys the relationship with the wheel and should be avoided. Most drivers like the open-backed soft leather gloves because their hands sweat and the ventilation is welcome.

Attention to your feet is important while driving, not only what you have on them but where you place them. Thick-soled shoes with little give in the ankle prevent you from feeling the pedals. Movements can become frantic down there and a little thought can spare you embarrassment. You need a shoe soft enough to give feel and pliant enough to allow for "heel and toe," or shifting and braking. Your feet know best, listen to them. Wear clothing that does not bind the body in movement. Billowing sleeves or long shoelaces can foul you up.

When you drive, forget all matters that take your mind off the business at hand, that is, driving that car. Support, comfort, familiarity, and ease of movement should be yours when you settle behind the wheel. If you are drunk, high, hung over, pissed at your wife or at the world, forget driving fast and turn up the stereo. An automobile is a tantalizing vehicle to get back at the world or to alleviate frustrations. It can also kill you.

3
THE OVERCARRIAGE

In the interest of brevity, let's lump together all those parts that the chassis supports and briefly run through a checklist to make sure all is in order. Some knowledge on the part of the reader is assumed so we'll pass over things lightly, trusting that if a question isn't answered fully you can do your own follow-up. The overcarriage contains all those parts that are not directly linked to the road; it is what you would call the "sprung weight."

We'll begin up front and our first concern is lights. Headlights can do more than light the way. At night they serve as a far better warning system than a horn when someone starts to creep out from a side road. They can also warn a car that you're overtaking. Turn indicators let the other drivers around you know your intentions better than does an arm stuck out the window.

Americans don't use their lights as much or as well as their European brothers do and that's a shame. This lack of expertise prevents us from making use of the advances in headlight technology that can nearly double nighttime vision. Use of high-intensity replacement units is prohibited in some states because Americans have a penchant for misusing their high beams. Nevertheless, headlights should be aimed regularly. When high beams are activated, you should get a good spread down the road. When dipped, the beams should not only drop in intensity but also to the right side of the road. That's where you should look, incidentally, when the dummy coming the other way forgets to dip his beams. It is also a common fault to "overdrive" the headlight beams. If you can't stop within your beams' farthest reaches, you're going too fast for the conditions.

Fog lights are a good idea and should be mounted as close to the roadway as possible without creating a hazard for yourself. Poor visibility and driving, at any speed, don't mix. In fog or heavy snow, be sure to run on low beams. High beams throw light into the fog or snow and create a "whiteout" which lowers visibility.

Sharing the grille with the lamps is the radiator. The cooling system comes in for extra loading when you drive hard. Check it frequently and thoroughly. Anti-freeze solutions give better cooling in summer months as well as being indispensable during the winter. It isn't unusual to throw a belt when the engine turns at higher rpm. You should make certain belts have the proper tension. Belts (and all other rubber fittings, like radiator hoses) deteriorate with age, and you can spot impending trouble and correct it by going over the engine compartment looking for cracks and signs of wear in the rubber components. There is a lot more plumbing today because of all the power assists and antipollution devices that fill up the engine bay.

Considerable power and efficiency have been lost because of the pollution-control devices now being fitted to all new cars. It is against the law in some states to exceed the amount of emittants considered normal for that motor. Engine modifications can do just that. Two things should guide you if you are about to alter the configuration of the engine: your wallet and your conscience.

The list of available parts to increase engine power and efficiency is almost endless. In fact, you have so many choices that any attempt to list them here would be foolish. In general, however, an engine should draw fuel/air mixture easily, fire efficiently, and convert energy into maximum motive force. Anything that makes the engine's task easier to accomplish is going to work to your benefit, from headers to balancing, from hotter sparking to a cleaner intake manifold.

It is important to understand that the engine, during high-performance levels, operates throughout a broad rpm spectrum, ranging from its mid to upper revolution capacities. Any modifications you envision should be done with an eye to getting the most power through the widest possible rpm band. This range is called the power band.

Check your owner's manual for the engine speed where horsepower and torque are maximized.

If an engine works hard, it builds up more heat, and this heat negatively affects the plugs, points, and oil. Frequent checks of these three factors can improve the life expectancy of your engine.

Your link to all that power, the throttle linkage, should work easily and have a positive return spring. A runaway engine is truly dangerous.

In addition to that "seat of the pants" feeling, your gauges will keep you posted on the status of your engine. Warning lights may be fine for the average motorist but for hard driving you should have gauges fitted. Water temperature, oil temperature, and oil pressure are the big three behind the tachometer.

Right behind the engine (usually) is the transmission. It has to be the least understood part of an automobile. The transmission is mated to the engine through the clutch and the pressure plate that works against the flywheel. In an automatic transmission, this coupling is accomplished by a fluid medium that acts on two turbinelike wheels, one on the flywheel, the other linked to the imput shaft of the transmission.

The function of the transmission, automatic or manual, is to deliver engine power to the rear wheels in the most efficient manner possible. It accomplishes this purpose by altering the ratio between engine imput and transmission output through a series of gears, first being the lowest (highest numerically, or the greatest multiplication), and the top gear, the highest (lowest numerically, or least multiplication).

An automatic requires little maintenance unless you spot leakage or the shifts become sloppy or, worse yet, fail to occur. A check of your driveway will warn of any leaks and oil-level checks are simple to perform. Unlike engine oil, the motor must be running to check the transmission oil level. If the oil is low and topping the transmission doesn't last, it's time to see the transmission doctor. Automatics are sophisticated pieces of equipment, and only trained and highly competent specialists are qualified to work on them.

If you're going to be driving in a spirited fashion, it is best to work with a manual transmission. Power loss is minimal and complete control is exercised by the driver and not by the transmission. Automatics have a way of picking their own moment to shift. In manuals, signs of trouble announce themselves readily.

The linkage should be precise and the transmission free from clunks and groans and those nerve-grating grinds that tell of trouble in the making. Most manufacturers offer heavy-duty clutch and transmission options and it's best to fit them. Special shifting linkages are also a smart move. It is no fun to drive a balky transmission. Shifting procedures and learning to take it easy on the transmission will be discussed in a later chapter. Here we're only concerned that the mechanics of your car work as well as they should. The transmission is vital.

Make sure your clutch isn't slipping and that it works easily. Heat kills clutches, and since they work on the friction principle, too much clutch slippage only shortens their life.

The integrity of your braking system should also be checked out. Make sure the fluid levels are right up to the mark.

Moving back from the transmission we come to the drive shaft, just about the dullest link in the power train. It seldom gives trouble and needs little maintenance, although you should keep an ear open for those telltale clunks that can warn of wear at the universal joints.

Connected to the other end of the drive shaft is the differential. It takes a tremendous beating and rarely protests. It must absorb hundreds of horsepower and transmit this power at right angles through the axles to the rear wheels. You must respect the engineering that has gone into its design because a differential accomplishes its task with very little power loss. Some differentials also contain a transmission, and they are called, oddly enough, transaxles. Mid-engined or rear-engined cars have this setup.

Unfortunately, most differentials send power only to the right rear wheel. If you have this arrangement, you should consider switching to a limited-slip differential, which delivers power to both rear wheels. Besides the 100 per cent increase in power delivery, a limited-slip rear end makes allowances for the different rotational speeds assumed by the opposing rear tires when going around a turn. The outside tire has farther to roll and the limited-slip differential takes this into account.

Out from the differential we have the axles, which are really just small drive shafts. They do their task with little fuss. On cars with independent rear suspensions, the differential housing is fixed to the chassis and does not move, which means that the axles have to be articulated. This articulation can be by means of universal joints or metalastic doughnuts. Swing axles, transaxles, or other independent applications need more care and attention.

The last assumption we must make about the readiness of the overcarriage to do its part is that all the body panels are securely fastened. Hopefully, you have a taut ship. Now for the undercarriage.

4
THE UNDERCARRIAGE

The underside of your car doesn't receive the attention it deserves, primarily because there haven't been many advances, at least in American designs, over the past few years. For some reason Detroit hasn't kept pace with the rest of the world. For instance, we are just beginning to see the spread of disk-brake applications even though disks came out in the fifties and were clearly superior. The same point could be made with the Wankel engine or radial tires. Be that as it may, our present point of focus is the undercarriage of your automobile. The logical beginning is the frame.

Everything is attached to the frame and it helps to think of it as a skeleton. In most cases you will be stuck with whatever type of frame is hidden under the body. Chassis modifications are extremely expensive. About the only low-cost improvement you can make to a frame is the installation of a roll bar.

The three open areas in a car, engine bay, passenger compartment, and trunk, keep a frame from supplying total rigidity. A roll bar not only stiffens the frame but keeps your car off your head if you turn turtle. Roll bars work; and anyone honestly considering high-speed driving, particularly the race-track variety, where their use is mandatory, should have one installed, using the best material and finest workmanship possible. It may have to work only once, but a failed roll bar usually means you won't get another chance.

Attached to the frame are the suspension members. The suspension has a difficult task to perform. Its job is to locate the wheels and tires in their most advantageous posture, which means upright and perpendicular to the road throughout the length of suspension travel.

Up front we must also have a capacity for steering. Almost all manufacturers use an independent suspension up front so each tire, though connected by the tie rods, works independently of the other. Provisions also must be made for suspension adjustments of toe-in, toe-out, caster, and camber.

In the rear, the situation is not quite so complicated since the wheels aren't steered and deal only with power and up and down movements. The usual application (though this will change slowly) is a live rear end. "Live" means simply that power is transmitted through the suspension member, that is, the differential and axles, including the housing. With a live rear end, the wheels are kept perpendicular to the road by the rigidity of the design. Unfortunately, this means that a bump under one wheel is transmitted to the other side of the car. In effect, it's a huge anti-roll bar. Independent rear suspensions are also available and their design can be quite sophisticated. In independent systems the object is to isolate road shocks from being transmitted to the other corners.

The springing medium may be coil springs, leaf springs (called semielliptic and mounted either fore and aft or transversely), torsion bars, or hydraulic. Each, properly designed, can give excellent results. Working in conjunction with the shock absorbers, almost any springing medium can take the hard knocks out of driving.

Since the tires also have flex characteristics they figure into the suspension system too, but we'll discuss tires in the next chapter. Briefly, your tires soak up most of the small irregularities in the road. When the tires' limits are reached, then the springs take over.

The weight of the car as it rests on the suspension parts means that the springing medium is preloaded, or partially compressed. When you hit a big bump the suspension is forced up (compression) and the springs soften the shock. Then, the springing medium has to force the wheel back down onto the road (rebound). The springs, as you can see, have a great deal of work to do. No spring does this job without waste. This wasted energy is absorbed by the shock absorbers. Shocks control the action of the springs and, through the springing medium, the wheels.

A shock absorber does this by the action of its cylinder. A heavy fluid is forced through a series of orifices that choke back the full flow so it reacts to jounce and rebound forces more slowly and in a more controlled fashion than any spring action. Thus, the wheels don't hop up and down uncontrollably. Heavy-duty shocks are better able to throw off heat and thereby exercise more control.

Springs and shocks, by changing the energy of the suspension travel from movement to heat, need a constant flow of air to operate efficiently. You can easily determine the condition of your shocks by bouncing once on the bumper. If the car rocks repeatedly, the shocks need replacement. Cars with bad shocks wallow in their own surplus energy.

A suspension system is carefully thought out and tampering with it can upset the geometry and handling characteristics of the car. Gimmicks such as jacking up the front or raising the rear with blocks and other such rot are downright deadly, besides looking asinine. Raising the ends alters the center of gravity and the center of gravity is important to getting around quickly. With the fanny up in the air, the guy following you has a really good shot at bursting your gas tank.

Lowering a car, though it would appear to lower the center of gravity, can also negatively affect cornering ability since it limits the travel built in to the suspension. Then, too, we have all had to straddle that piece of metal in the middle of our lane. Think about that hole in your oil pan if you don't have adequate ground clearance.

The center of gravity is that point where the weight of the entire automobile is centered, and all the forces that act on a car act through this point. It is also that point from which weight shifts forward or back on braking or acceleration. It is capable of moving. That is important to understand.

The static weight distribution (a car at rest) determines the center of gravity in the horizontal plane. The vertical distribution of weight (from road to roof) determines the height of the center of gravity from the roadway. Where these centers of mass intersect, you find the center of gravity. There are forces, however, that can alter the center of gravity. When you go around a turn, weight is shifted from the inside tires to the outside tires. In acceleration, weight shifts backward. When you brake, the weight shifts forward and the nose dips.

The engine is the heaviest single piece of equipment on your car and its location usually determines where in the horizontal plane the center of mass is positioned. The fore and aft weight distribution is important to handling since centrifugal force wants to act through the center of gravity. When it is located forward of the mid-line of the car, centrifugal force acts most strongly on the front wheels. The reverse is true when the center of gravity lies aft of the mid-line.

This gives rise to three terms you should understand: understeer, oversteer, and neutral handling. Understeer is the tendency of the car to require more steering imput to negotiate a turn as the speed is increased. Oversteer is, of course, the opposite, or the tendency of a car to require less steering influence to negotiate a corner when the speed is increased. Neutral handling means that the steering influence necessary to go around a corner is little changed as the speed goes up.

We have seen that the weight of a car shifts so it is obvious that a car will react differently in different situations. In later chapters, we will see how we can use these forces to our advantage.

The last link in the suspension system, although it has nothing to do with suspending the car, is the brake system.

Brakes have an awesome job to perform and most all of the modern combinations do a pretty fine job. Drum brakes are more common in America although we're finally getting around to recognizing the superiority of disks. In drum applications, the drum turns with the wheel and has two shoes, semielliptic in shape, which are securely mounted and press outward on the inner surface of the turning drum. Through friction, they convert the motion energy to heat. In disks, a disk turns with the wheel (or is sometimes mounted on the axles in what is called "inboard disks") and calipers, again securely mounted, press inward on the spinning disk in a clamplike motion to lower the speed. Disk or drum, both work on friction principles to change the kinetic energy of a moving body into heat which must then be dissipated into the airstream. Getting more air to the brakes increases their efficiency. Because disk brakes are more exposed to the airstream, they work more efficiently. Also, disks wipe themselves free of dirt and/or water, which, next to heat, are the biggest enemies of brake function.

Most auto manufacturers offer high-performance brake options and they are best for heavy duty use since the brake pads, or shoes, have more resistance to heat fade.

When you add the tires and rims to the brakes, springs, shock absorbers, axles and differential (if they move), you have what is called the "unsprung weight." This unsprung weight also includes the locating links of the suspension. Inertia plays an important role in handling and it is well to remember that the more weight you have in motion, the more energy must be brought to bear to alter inertia. In suspension systems, this means that the heavier the moving parts (unsprung weight), the more force necessary to put those members back into position. The less the unsprung weight, the more control the suspension can exert.

Study photos 21 and 22, showing head-on views of a sedan and a Formula car. Notice in these pictures how the weight mass of the open wheel race car, besides being obviously lower, is centered beneath the mid-line of the tires and between the wheels. In this way the weight of the car moves through the tires rather than rolling over the top. Here the effects of shifting weight are minimized to the maximum degree. Technically speaking, the race car has a very low polar movement. Formula cars represent the peak of the automotive "state of the art," and while we will never have this type of car on our roads, it is nice to see just how far we have already gone.

Suspension systems are designed to withstand the tremendous loadings imposed by road shocks. Their business is to keep the wheels located properly at all times by counteracting the various forces that act on a car. Suspension design is a very complicated business and tampering with these basics should be done only after careful research.

We have now briefly covered the entire car from stem to stern and from top to bottom. It's time now to move to the most direct link between you and the road, your tires.

5
TIRES: THE CRITICAL LINK

Place your hand on a flat surface with fingers spread wide. Multiply by four the area covered and you have roughly the amount of road area covered by your tires, and those 150-odd square inches are the most important single element in driving, particularly high-performance driving.

Through the contact patch all the forces that act on a car must find their realization, from turning to braking to acceleration. When that contact area is reduced, so also is the performance of the car. If it ceases to exist (as in the tire leaving the ground), all control is lost. For a tire to operate at peak efficiency, it must be rolling at a rate consistent with the speed of the car and must be perpendicular to the roadway with the full amount of available tread area forced down on the road.

A tire operates below maximum when it is sliding or skidding, is presented at a severe angle to the direction of travel, is overinflated or underinflated, or when the surface it is running on has poor abrasive qualities. It must dispel 120 gallons of water per minute at 60 miles per hour in heavy rain, provide resistance to sideslip for cornering power, and be able to withstand the abuse of speed, heat build-up, and the shock of road hazards. Tires do more work than any other part of your car.

A positive indicator of the worth of racing, vis-à-vis tire development, has come from the hotly contested battles waged over three continents by the world's leading tire manufacturers. As a case in point, the speeds at Indianapolis have increased dramatically over the past ten years from 150.370 mph by Parnelli Jones in 1962 to 195.940 mph by Bobby Unser in 1972. Qualifying speed at Indy in 1973 came within a whisker of breaking the 200-mph barrier. Improved tires are the main reason for this speed increase. Remember the frantic pit stops in days gone by? They may still be wild and woolly, but not for tires. Modern racing tires not only stick better, they last longer, too.

The men who design the cars for Indy have taken advantage of tire performance by creating suspension systems that can make the most out of this new capacity. Additionally, the slippery shape of the rear-engined layout and newfound power have a lot to do with the increased speeds. But any observer will attest to the importance of tires. With wings and airfoils keeping the weight on the tires, the speeds have become phenomenal. The speeds have increased as much in the past ten years as they did in the previous forty-one! The reason is the increased width and the art of designing in high hysteresis (the actual grip of the tire to a surface) with prolonged wear expectancy.

These advances are already filtering down to ordinary tires with the appearance of wider tires and now the radials. It is not beyond reason to expect 40,000 miles with belted radials, and this mileage bonus is coming to us with greater stability, road-holding ability, and better poor-surface characteristics than even thought possible ten years ago.

Quantum leaps have been made in tread design, rubber compounds, and in carcass construction. The wide tires spread the weight of the vehicle over a larger area. Radial construction keeps the number-one enemy of tires—heat—down to more advantageous limits by reducing the amount of internal friction. And better suspensions are being designed to incorporate these newfound capacities.

The biggest bargain in the automotive field is not the "economy" tires of yesteryear but the top-of-the-line "premium" tires. On a cost-per-mile basis they so far outstrip ordinary tires that most manufacturers have done away with economy grades. Without question, premium tires are the best insurance you can buy. It pays to buy the best, period.

An extensive look at tires would take a book of its own. Here I'll discuss their role as they relate to high-performance driving. The tires are the most important function of high-speed driving because if you understand their operation—how they best perform—you have gone a long way toward mastering your automobile.

There is a wide variety of road surfaces and you face diverse conditions when you drive. You may, in the course of a day, find yourself on ice, sand, in water, or on smooth dry concrete. Unless you have a car built for a specific purpose (dragster or dune buggy) you want a tire that does the best job over the widest spectrum of surface possibilities. That tire, not unexpectedly, is the belted radial. For sheer over-all performance, it can't be beaten.

Heat, the tire destroyer, builds up as the sidewall and carcass deflect when the tread runs over the road. Road shocks and cornering also create more heat. The normal method of tire construction is called "bias." In this application, the reinforcing cords are run at an angle from edge to edge, usually around 70 degrees. Cord angles have steadily decreased over the years and the appearance of the radials take this decrease even further. Radial cords run bead to bead, or from rim edge to rim edge, at an angle of about 8 degrees. Because the cords don't cross over each other, internal friction is greatly reduced. The belts that can be found on both radials and newer bias tires run under the tread in the direction of rotation and this keeps the tread presented in its most efficient manner, flat and in full contact across the entire width of the "footprint." These belts also increase penetration resistance.

The sidewall is the connecting medium between tread and rim. It is in the sidewall that cornering force is generated as it flexes under side loads. Radial construction allows for the sidewall to do as much as possible, providing for more controlled flexing while keeping the tread running flat.

Let's consider how a tire generates traction. First, of course, is the surface on which it is running. The more abrasive the surface, the better the tire will stick. Ice has a coefficient of traction factor less than 10 per cent of dry concrete. To give you an idea of the esoteric nature of tire performance, even the temperature of ice has a bearing on tire capability.

Next is the nature of the rubber compound used. Hysteresis describes the actual bite, or grip, of the tire. A high-hysteresis tire "clings" to the road and requires more power to effect rotation as the tread actually has to be pulled off the roadway. High-hysteresis tires give more traction but they wear faster, as you might expect. Manufacturers have worked out a compromise between long mileage and superior traction.

Weight also affects traction characteristics. The more weight on a tire, the better the traction. But it is a double-edged sword. More weight also means more rolling resistance and that means more heat. Weight also must be considered in the total performance of the car. More weight means more power must be generated by the tire to overcome the greater effects of inertia.

I have discussed how weight can shift on a chassis and this weight transfer is conferred on the tire. In braking, weight shifts forward and the front tires have more load and consequently more available traction. On acceleration, weight shifts backward. In cars with rear-wheel drive this is to your benefit since the rear tires need more weight for increased traction.

When the tire is turned out of its plane of rotation, it produces lateral resistance. This is a difficult process to explain. A tire turned out of its plane of rotation would be a tire that is being steered off a straight path or a tire that is presented at an angle to the road's surface and the direction of travel.

Turned out of its plane of rotation, a tire begins to distort in relationship to the wheel, or rim, so that the wheel takes a path outside of the one taken by the tread. This occurs at all speeds above near zero. The sidewall must flex to accommodate this offset. In resisting this displacement, power is generated through the sidewall to counteract centrifugal force which, acting through the car's center of gravity, wants to take the car to the outside of a turn. This displacement, or offset, occurs on both front and rear tires.

No car at speed really follows the true path as taken by the tread. Some slippage is always present when the tire is angled, or presented to the roadway at an angle. Up to certain limits, the greater the deflec-

Tire Deflection

10°
Slip
Angle

True Direction

FIGURE 1

FIGURE 2

tion of the wheel to the straight-ahead angle of attack, the greater the resistance of the sidewall and the more lateral resistance a tire has. This is true up to about 10 degrees for a radial tire and somewhat more, 15 degrees, in a bias tire.

Between 0 degrees and 10 degrees (or more, depending on the tire) a tire will perform its best. The angle of deflection—where the tire goes and where it is actually being pointed—is called the "slip angle." Its function is most important. If you exceed the slip angle designed by the tire and chassis engineers, you will suffer a dramatic loss of total available traction. In physical terms, you can expect to spin out or plow off the road.

Figures 1 and 2 illustrate sidewall deflection and slip angle parameters.

The newer wide tires and radials have less slip angle built in and so a new style of driving has come into being. At one time, race drivers could throw their cars around quite a bit without suffering undue loss of traction, but that's changed. Cars are being built to be *driven* around turns, not tossed around. This means that any alteration of the car's attitude in reference to its direction of travel should not exceed the maximum slip angle for the tires. In the old days you could tell who was really getting it on by how much the tail was hung out. Today, when you see a car in that posture you know the driver is losing efficiency.

A tire with a lower aspect ratio (more width) has, generally, more sidewall stiffness. This stiffness determines how much force will be generated at a certain slip angle. At the same force level a stiffer tire will therefore have a smaller slip angle. For example, an H-size radial tire on a 15-inch rim, inflated to 28 lbs psi and loaded with 1,510 pounds, will have different stiffness rates according to its aspect ratio.

Aspect Ratio	Cornering Stiffness (lb/deg)
60	248
70	226
78	178

The aspect ratios of the tires on Indy cars are below 40! Imagine how much lateral resistance they can generate.

A tire can provide only so much traction and during cornering this total available traction must be divided, some going to lateral resistance, some for acceleration or braking. Just holding a car at a steady rate of speed during cornering soaks up a percentage of total available traction. Taking all the variables into account that are under the driver's control—weight, deflection, braking, or accelerating—you can see how complicated things become. The forces acting on the tires, just to make matters worse, are different for each corner of the car. Consider the wheels and tires as two units: the rear tires and wheels and the front tires and wheels. Each set of tires behaves differently. Each set has its own slip angle.

A car is said to understeer when the slip angle for the front tires is greater than the rear. A car will oversteer when the rear tires have the greater slip angle. In most designs today, engineers have built in understeer, which gives the greatest sense of security to most drivers who feel more comfortable when controlling things at the front of the car.

A car with severe understeer will require more turning influence to get through a given turn when the speed is increased. The reverse is true for an oversteering machine. An understeering car tends to scrub off speed in a more predictable manner than an oversteering car.

"Scrubbing" occurs any time the tire is turned off line. Tires require the least amount of energy when they are running straight ahead. They use up considerably more power not only to increase speed but just to maintain speed when they are turned. You can see this for yourself by holding a steady throttle foot when you go through a turn. You will find that your speed is lowered. The sharper the turn (more tire deflection) the more the speed will be scrubbed off. Most drivers do not apply power when the car goes into a turn. The wheel, deflected and using up more energy, therefore "scrubs off" total car speed. When the speed is great and the front tires are turned too sharply, all directional control is lost and the car slides right on. This effect is called "plowing." The most helpless feeling in the world results when the front end "washes out," or leaves you sliding straight on with the front tires cocked at a severe angle. There is nothing you can do but get the front tires straightened out and hope you aren't already off the road.

When the rear tires exceed their optimum slip angle you still can exercise some control because the front tires are sticking. A car that is "plowing" (front tires angled past their slip angle) can be controlled, however, by breaking the traction of the rear tires, causing them to assume a larger slip angle. This will be discussed in more detail in a later chapter.

Braking or accelerating reduces the resistance to sideslip because the total amount of traction available is being split. It follows then that the most efficient form of cornering would be when no braking or accelerating influences are added. But the highest possible cornering speed is not always what we are after. In fact, it is seldom important. The split tire function does tell us, however, that when we want the most efficient acceleration or braking we will do those in as straight a line as possible or make allowances for the limitations of the tire.

At 60 miles an hour, assuming a tire diameter of 25 inches, a tire makes approximately 13 revolutions per second. A tire's traction is limited by the relative velocity of tread to surface. When the differential exceeds roughly 15 per cent, tire performance falls off. Thus, a locked wheel in braking has nearly 100 per cent velocity differential between tread velocity and the road. Not very efficient! Similarly, a wildly spinning wheel when the car is at rest (as in coming off the line while drag racing) has very nearly 100 per cent velocity differential. Also not very efficient. The sum of the preceding demonstrates the importance of keeping the wheel rolling at a rate consistently within 15 per cent of the actual difference between tread velocity and the road.

At speeds above 10 miles an hour, more or less, the tire, even in a straight line with no torque added, is slipping. As the speed increases, this slippage becomes more pronounced. It isn't unusual for a car to run out of traction at really high speeds. In that case, no matter how much power is on tap, the car cannot attain a faster speed because the power is not transferred to the ground because of the slippage.

In cornering, the relative velocity of the tread to the surface is at an angle, or tangent. The faster the tread is forced over the ground, the less traction you have. At higher speeds, then, a tire delivers less traction.

In cornering, the sidewall attempts to bring the deflected wheel back directly over the tread. The wheel, remember, is running outside the path as taken by the tread. This aligning action can be called torque. This torque can be readily felt in cars without power steering as it is transmitted back through the steering mechanism to the steering wheel where it is felt by the driver. The experienced driver can tell how much lateral resistance the tires are providing by the "feel" of the wheel. The better power-steering units also transmit this torque back to the driver, albeit somewhat more subtly.

The practical aspect of the discussion of tread velocity may be summed up as follows: You do not want to lock up the wheels in braking. You do not want to set the rear wheels spinning wildly on acceleration. You do not want to exceed an angle of more than 15 degrees (10 degrees for a radial tire) when you corner. The handling characteristics of your car will change as the speed is increased, particularly the understeering car. At higher speeds a great deal of the rear tires' tractive abilities is being taken up by the torque being fed into them, consequently they will assume a more decided tendency toward sideslip. An oversteering car's normal characteristics will be exaggerated.

It is the relative velocity between the tire and the ground that is important. Under acceleration, the tire is moving over the road faster than the car; in braking, the relative velocity of tire to ground speed is slower. In cornering, the relative velocity of the tire is at a slip angle to the direction of rotation.

The forces acting on the total car are measured in g's, that is, percentiles of gravity whose force is always called acceleration, or 32 feet per second. A tire produces its power in three planes: braking (deceleration), traction (acceleration), and cornering force (lateral resistance). The following chart will give you an idea what percentages you can expect in dry and wet weather.

	DRY	WET
Braking	.7 g's	.3 g's
Traction	.7 "	.5 "
Cornering	.7 "	.15 "

If you ask a tire to perform within its boundaries, you get the best results, and they can be very good indeed.

It is important that the tires be matched. Radial tires should not be used in conjunction with normal or bias tires. They are fundamentally different and mixing sets of tires can harm your car's handling rather than improve it. If you're going to radials, go all the way and fit four.

As we move through the following chapters you will see how to get the best out of your tires. Due to the advances in tire design, if you are using all that tires have to offer, you are really cooking.

6
SHIFTING

Automation has led us away from the manual transmission and the technique of shifting has been lost to many drivers. The pleasures in shifting, the fun and the craft, more than make up for the extra work.

With a manual you decide exactly what gear you'll be in and there are no two ways about it. It permits the driver to keep the engine turning in its power band by altering the ratio of engine revolutions to wheel revolutions through the use of three or more possible gearing combinations. Between each gear there is a set difference between engine and wheel speed and that is called the "spread." One of the driver's first tasks is to find out what the spreads are.

Checking the spreads is pretty easy. Hold the car speed steady at 4,000 rpm in first gear. Check the speedometer. Without losing or gaining speed, shift into second gear and make a note of the rpm difference between the two. The rpm differential is the spread. It may be 800 rpm or more depending on the type of transmission. Close ratio transmissions have less spread between gears. In a like manner, check out the spread between second and third. And then check third and fourth and fourth and fifth if you have them. You should know these spreads not only through your intellect and mathematical ability but also through feel. There isn't always time to check the tach.

The spread will be most important when I discuss downshifting because matching engine and wheel speed during downshifts keeps the power flowing smoothly, and smoothness is a key word in high-performance driving.

Modern transmissions have synchromesh cones that act much like mini-clutches to help match the speed of the gears as they relate to each other inside the gearbox. While most synchromesh transmissions can do the job of matching gear speeds and do it quite well, that still leaves you with the engine speed to be concerned about. A shift, up or down, that is accompanied by a lurch or a balk is not an efficient gear change. You can, it's true, just pull into the next gear, let the clutch pedal out, and let the synchro rings do all the dirty work. But if you feel the engine rpm go up and the car speed go down you have not made a good shift. Besides that, the transmission has to do what you can do yourself. A transmission has enough to do as it is and anything you can do to lessen its work load will be translated into many more miles of trouble-free driving.

Shifting up (from first to second, second to third, and so on) is easy and most drivers do it well. If you don't try to force things, the gearbox will generally drop right into the next cog and you can press on. The timing of the normal upshift should allow the engine speed to run down to match the next higher gear. Knowing your spreads helps here too. Try to shift so each gear change is hardly felt.

Most people downshift in the following rhythm. Clutch pedal in, pull to the next lower gear with an accompanying whine as the gear-box matches the speed, then clutch pedal out, which makes the engine run up to speed with deceleration because of the effects of engine compression. There are better ways. In fact, there are three better ways.

After you've selected your next lower gear and just before you let the clutch pedal out, run the engine up to speed. (You will know how much if you've checked the spreads.) Now this method is better than the former illustration but it still makes the transmission do a lot of unnecessary work. Let's double clutch.

Double clutching requires an extra movement of the clutch pedal and a small hesitation between gear selections as the lever passes through the "neutral zone." Its purpose is to match all the turning items—wheels, transmission, and engine—so there is no break in the flow of power and the strain on the gearbox is reduced.

In double clutching you pause briefly in the throw between gears while in neutral. During this pause you let the clutch pedal out for a moment as you give the throttle a "bump," bringing the engine speed up to match the spread, then push in the clutch pedal quickly and select your gear. When you let the clutch pedal back out you shouldn't feel any hitch. Using this method of downshifting takes the loading off the transmission synchros.

Usually you are gearing down for an impending corner which may also require braking. There is a way to do both operations, shifting and braking, in one action and it is called "heel and toe." It is exactly the same as double clutching except the right foot is angled so that the toe is on the brake pedal and the heel is on the throttle. Depending on pedal location and the size of your feet, it may be you have to use toe and heel, or, as was the case in a couple of cars I've owned, toe and ankle. Here's where the importance of those soft, pliant shoes pays off. It is a hard process to define in words so let's run through the pattern by the numbers.

For best results, start by angling your right foot so the toe is on the brake and the heel is touching the throttle. It feels odd at first but you'll get the hang of it. In this operation the brake, because you want to take speed off, is the most important, and the toe has more sensitivity than your heel. Here we go, step by step.

1. Lift your right foot from the accelerator as you reach for the gearshift lever.

2. Angle your right foot with the toe over the brake pedal.

3. Depress clutch pedal as you touch toe of right foot to brake pedal.

4. While clutch is disengaged, pull shift lever into neutral.

5. Without lifting or losing touch with the brake pedal, let the clutch pedal out briefly as you press your heel down on the throttle, "blipping" the engine as you press your heel down in a short motion.

6. Release gas pedal (it should only be a short poke) as you depress the clutch pedal again and pull into the gear you want. You then release the clutch.

In practice you ought to finish your shifting just as it is time to get off the binders and turn into the corner. There are a few things to keep in mind when you practice. The "blip" of the throttle should only take an instant. Too long and you run the risk of overrevving the engine. In neutral, with no loading, that can put a few holes in the engine. Also, remember you are braking as you shift so the rpm spread will not be as large as if you were maintaining speed.

Once you've mastered the mechanics of heel and toe without tying up the muscles and losing your cool, it is time to learn how to feel your brakes even as you blip the engine. You should be able to brake as hard as possible without locking up any wheel, match engine speed, and get into the next gear smoothly and effortlessly.

Integrating the shifting and braking time leaves you with more free time to control the car through the corner.

As a matter of course you should pay strict attention to every shift even while driving in traffic. Work hard to make your shifts almost imperceptible. In a week's time you should be able to shift up without a hitch, double clutch on all downshifts that don't require braking (as in coming to a light about to change), and perform the heel-and-toe maneuver almost without thinking about it.

There are several techniques you should develop that are a part of using your car wisely. While sitting at a light make it a practice to leave the car in neutral with the clutch engaged (pedal out). This takes the strain off the throw-out bearing. One other tip while waiting for that light: keep your eye on the rear-view mirror in case some idiot doesn't look like he's going to stop. It's a good habit to ease into a gear when a car approaches you from behind. Being able to leap forward even a small amount can help you avoid an accident or make that rear-end collision less injurious for all concerned. In other situations, however, make it a habit to always have the proper gear, the one that will allow you to accelerate should the need arise. Coasting along with the transmission in neutral is just asking for trouble.

In summary, shifting should be done quickly, cleanly, and above all, positively. Wishy-washy shifting has no place in a car that's going to be driven hard. Double clutching and heel and toe are not difficult habits to acquire and being familiar with the gearbox will allow you to know whether that shift you just missed was your fault or something mechanical.

For those of you who have an automatic transmission, things are done differently, although the object, as in the manual, is to achieve smooth shifts so the balance of the car isn't upset. The left foot becomes the braking foot and that isn't bad at all.

If you have a shifting quadrant mounted on the steering column, things can get a bit ticklish since you can't always find the correct slot. A center-console-mounted shift lever fares somewhat better because the stops are usually more clearly defined.

In overriding the automatic features of the transmission, care should be taken so the red line of the engine isn't exceeded. Make allowances for the lag time between shifts by moving the lever a few hundred revolutions below the red line when shifting up. In this fashion you make sure the red line and the engine remain intact.

For downshifting, anticipate the shift since there is a time lag between the selection of a gear and its engagement. Being familiar with the timing of your automatic is important. For a straight downshift where brakes are not applied, pull into the lower gear but only after you've made sure the red line won't be exceeded. When the transmission begins its shift, pop the throttle so the wheel speed and engine speed are matched. For some automatics you may have to endure a slight leap forward.

When you are on the brakes (left foot), be especially careful that you don't pick up too many revs. The car speed is being reduced by braking and the spread is diminished proportionately.

Shifting linkages are set up for all shifts to occur in order, 1, 2, 3, 4 or 4, 3, 2, 1. Ordinary usage sets wear patterns on the levers. Besides, that is normal for the driver, too. You get into a pattern and it is hard to break. Sometimes, however, situations demand a gear two stops lower than fourth, for instance. A hard turn at the end of a long straight can mean getting down two notches. You have several options.

You can use the compression of the engine to help you slow by using third gear before you go into second applying the heel-and-toe technique. Or you can put the lever in neutral and forget about third, matching engine speed for the spread between fourth and second. Or you can do the easy thing and keep your personal rhythm intact by going through third gear but not letting the clutch pedal out until you blip the engine prior to going into second. A transmission that works perfectly will sometimes balk at this because of its wear pattern, just as the driver, who has spent long hours perfecting his shifting technique, also may balk because of *his* wear patterns.

Some cars require a great deal of shifting to achieve maximum performance levels while others don't particularly care. The object in every shift is to keep the engine in the rpm range that best suits your next demand. There are enough surprises in driving as it is. Make precise shifting a part of your driving repertoire so that a missed shift isn't one of those surprises.

Always leave yourself a margin for error. Stirling Moss called it the "99 per cent." There is nothing left after 100 per cent. Keep a couple of hundred revs in hand and don't try to beat the transmission. One of the best ways to put a limit on your shifting speed is to make full use of the clutch travel. All the way in, all the way out.

The word "habit" has appeared several times in this chapter and it ought to be qualified. It isn't a good policy to do something in an automobile out of sheer habit. The mind should be controlling every aspect of driving, and all driver actions should be a response to a thought-out process. In other words, even though you are using what is a well-practiced action, it should be thought through before the event takes place. The distinction is important. Habits can be murderous. They are the reason that most accidents happen within a few miles of home.

7
THE STRAIGHT OF IT

Now that I have covered the car and the driver, it is time for a little practice. Where? Go to the drags.

The popularity of drag racing has created numerous small quarter-mile strips around the country and you can probably find one close to home. You don't necessarily want to go to one of the major tracks. You will be there to learn and the heat of competition can easily discourage you.

The two things you will be trying to learn are how to go fast in a straight line and how to stop quickly in a straight line. By taking advantage of the open track you can get both the sense and the feel of putting your car through its paces in comparative safety.

Few motorists know how well their car will stop because they seldom have the opportunity to test the brakes outside of a panic situation. Most of us know how the car will accelerate but we've never taken it out fully over a quarter of a mile. The cost of a day at the drags is low and the price of equipment damage, assuming you don't overcook it, is very low also.

Your attitude as you wheel into the track, pay your entrance fee, and get your car checked should be that of a novice, period. You are not there to pull down a class trophy (although strange things do happen) but to see how well you perform. You're there to find out how well the car responds to your wishes. Drag racing affords a unique opportunity to get your feet wet in the high-speed fraternity.

A drag strip is an ultrasafe place to get some sense of what it's all about. After the tech inspection you will be assigned a class. The next thing to do is park the car in the pits and go up to the bleachers to watch the goings-on. In this way you'll be able to check out the rhythm of drag racing. You'll be able to scout the approach lanes that you'll use to get to the staging area and you'll be able to follow the cars as they return to the paddock after their runs so you don't get lost after a run. If you take the time to sort it all out, you'll have most of the butterflies out of the way.

A day at the drags serves an important function. Remember that corners are connected by straights, and it is on the straight that a car performs best and makes the best time. You have to know how well your car "pulls" in each gear so passing situations can be analyzed completely before you pull out to pass and find out you don't have enough beans to do it in the time and space allowed. You also want to see how long it takes to haul all that weight down to manageable speeds, an important thing to know when you are approaching a corner at speed.

Leave the car as you drive it normally. Hub caps, however, should be removed as they have a tendency to spin off. Of course you've cleaned out the passenger compartment. Try to plan your journey to the strip so you arrive with less than a half tank of gas. The less gas you have on board the better it is for speed and safety reasons. The biggest and most feared enemy of a driver is fire. Gasoline really fuels a flame. Also, it adds weight to the car and more weight means less speed.

By placing a call to the strip before you go, you can make sure you are there for the practice or trial runs and not the actual races. This usually means morning. Get out there early and you'll have plenty of time and opportunity to get in the three runs you should be prepared for. The practice runs may be by class or on a first come, first run basis. Sit for a while and listen to the announcer. When your call comes and you feel you're ready, get in your car and drive *slowly* to the staging area. Don't be a pit racer. The speed should be left for the track.

If you happen to draw with another car, do what the pros do. Pay no attention to the car in the other lane. Do your own thing. You have plenty to worry about without confusing yourself or getting the adrenalin up.

Automatics, although somewhat slower than the same car with a manual, make the trip down the strip easier so we'll discuss automatics first.

After you pass the staging area you'll be sent to the line and asked to hold there. If, as you've noticed from the bleachers, cars are being waved off, rather than using the lights, take a moment to get yourself set, then torque up the transmission. That means holding the car with the left foot on the brake while the right foot feeds power to the engine. Don't go hog-wild on this. Holding or torquing like this is hard on the transmission. It builds up heat. Just feed in enough gas to make the car tremble under you and feel like it wants to jump off the line. Read the tach and use an rpm just below maximum torque: 2,500 to 3,000 rpm should suffice. Don't hold the car for longer than five seconds. If something happens, being waved off, for instance, let off the gas and put the transmission in neutral and wait for the flagman to direct you.

But if the man says go, do just that. On your first run let the automatic do all the work and forget about overriding the shift sequences. When you get the green light, release the brake foot and feed in just enough power to set the wheels to spinning. You don't have to worry about wheelspin if you don't have the power. A hot car, however, requires some restraint, especially in the first 50 feet. A tire, as we've seen, gives maximum accelerative ability when it is spinning just slightly faster than the car speed. This is not the same as in braking, where the tire must maintain rolling contact to perform best. Slight wheelspin coming off the line also keeps the revs up.

If your car doesn't have the power to break loose the rear tires when the shift to second occurs, keep your foot on the floor and run it out. If your car does have the power to break traction when it shifts, lift your foot slightly as the shift takes place. Check your tachometer at the shift points so you'll know how much you will be able to override the transmission on your next run. The automatics will generally shift a few hundred revolutions under the red line when on full automatic. When you pass through the traps, check your tach, not the speedometer. The traps are where your speed and ET (elapsed time) are tabulated. They are well marked so you'll know when to look at the rev counter.

With a manual transmission you'll have more to do going down the strip. It takes a lot of practice to come off the line with just the proper amount of wheelspin, to make each shift crisply, and at the same time to keep the car straight and the rpm below the red line. But practice is what you're there for.

When you move to the line, run the revolutions up to a speed just above the maximum torque and hold the engine at that speed. When the flag drops, drop the clutch quickly and move out. You may just let the clutch pedal out with a bang (hard on the power train) or feed in the clutch gradually depending on the amount of wheelspin and the drop in revolutions. Try to set up some wheelspin leaving the line because it keeps the revs where the power is. Remember, uncontrolled wheelspin just lessens tire efficiency. If you have a powerful car, plan on shifting up to second some 500 rpm below the red line. The time and speed lost are minuscule since most cars with power pull very well in the lower gears.

If you have read the charts for your car you know where maximum torque comes on and that should be your guide for takeoff revolutions. If the engine bogs down just after you leave the line you may want to try a higher engine speed. If that doesn't break the rear tires loose, plan on slipping the clutch a small amount on your next run. A car weighs anywhere from 2,000 to 4,000 pounds and getting all that weight into motion puts the engine, clutch, transmission, and differential to a mighty stiff test. There's no sense breaking something on these first runs so give the car the edge.

Any deviation from a straight-ahead path lowers your speed and increases your ET. Don't bang the shifts home or abuse the equipment. Smooth, swift, and precise movements of the gear lever will serve you better than mashing, bashing, and thrashing. Keep cool and go down the strip calmly. The car is supposed to do the work.

The first time I ran my 348 Pontiac at San Fernando Drag Strip, I missed all three shifts and felt like a fool. It isn't unusual to blow a shift when you're new to drag racing. Slow down a bit on the shifts and you'll get them home.

Try not to shift in the traps. That last shift can ruin your times and it shouldn't hurt the engine to overrev a few hundred r's in a higher gear. This of course is not the case if you see you are going to go over the red line by more than, say, 400 rpm. Two hundred revolutions won't blow the engine but a thousand will.

You've gotten both the automatic and the manual down the strip. Now what?

You'd better stop. When you pass the end of the traps run your speed out for a second, then get on the brakes, hard. Bring your speed down as fast as you can without locking up any wheel and keep the car on a straight line. If you feel a wheel locking, come off the brakes for a moment and try again. If you start to pull left or right, lighten up on your braking and get the car straight again. If the brakes begin to fade or the pedal pressure goes sky-high, relax your braking effort and give the brakes time to recover. If you're not slowing positively, pump the brakes in a series of applications until the speed drops.

The worst thing that can happen is complete brake failure. Should this happen, don't panic. The runout area will be long enough to get your speed down. The first thing to do is to let the air drag and rolling resistance take off what speed they can. Next, downshift to the next gear and let engine compression pull the speed down even further. Run down the gears, in sequence, and you'll be slowed enough to turn off. Get the car stopped before doing any investigative work. If the brakes come back, proceed slowly to the pits and park the car. If you can fix it, do it. If you can't, forget about driving anywhere until you get the anchors checked. There is usually someone in the pits to help so don't be afraid to ask.

Getting on the brakes hard at the end of the run doesn't mean a wild tire-smoking halt, but rather a smooth, steady, and rapid reduction of speed under full control. In this way you will experience for yourself one of the maxims of high-performance driving. It takes far less distance and time to STOP a car than it does to get up to speed.

When you come to a stop at the end of your run make a quick check out the window and mark your forward progress. An average American sedan may take 1,320 feet to get up to 80 miles an hour. It will stop in 300 feet. The reason is pretty simple. Four wheels supply braking; only two give you acceleration. You will see how important that is in later chapters.

A good set of brakes can produce an incredible amount of braking power. Brakes should bring you to a smooth in-line stop without shuddering, wheel hop, or lockup at any wheel. They should give you a good solid feeling and do their job with no fuss. It's important in these braking applications that you feel what each wheel is doing—how well it's sticking. If you lock up the wheels, you no longer have directional control and the braking distances go up dramatically. The first moment of braking is the most critical. On any highway you can see long black skid marks left by people who in that first moment of braking, either because of fear, surprise, or ignorance, pounded on the brake pedal, locked up the wheels, and slid along until they stopped or hit something. Don't stab at the brakes. Apply them.

Anyone who has seen a sports-car race knows that the men who know best about "slow power" never lock up the brakes. If they do, you're probably looking at an accident about to happen.

When you get back to the pits, pick up your time slip and save it for future reference. If it's an open session, take a breather and go over every aspect of your run down the strip. Did you get too much wheelspin? If so, lower your engine speed or slip the clutch slightly.

If you missed a shift (or even three), you know that you'll have to work on that part of your routine. It may be that the linkage is not set up for really crisp shifting. Many standard systems don't like to be pushed around. If you feel that's the problem, make allowances for it on your next run by slowing down your shifting speed with full clutch travel and exaggerated movements when you reach for the next gear.

Did your engine pull its best? You get a different feeling on a strip, and the engine that seemed to be running sweet on the street can come off awfully sour at a drag strip. If the engine balked, pinged, or otherwise acted up, perhaps you better forget the rest of the day's racing and make a note to get the car checked. You can really damage an engine that isn't running right, particularly if you press it.

If you went over the rev limit, you know you have to pay more attention to the tach. Once you know the feelings and sounds of your engine at peak revs you can pay less attention to the tachometer.

Beyond the mechanics of getting the car down the chute, you have now had a chance to feel the car's acceleration and braking. Did you notice how the power from the engine seemed to swell as the revolutions came up to peak horsepower? Could you sense how much grip the tires had? Did you feel the steering get "light" as the speed increased? These are some of the feelings you'll want to remember.

If, after going over your performance and that of your car, and you feel up to it, get back for another dose. When you have completed three runs, you should have enough data to carry you for a while. On the other hand, you may want to run in your class and find out what your car will do with others in the same class. If you decide to run again, good luck. If not, grab a hot dog and watch the rest of the day's activities.

Compare your timing slips. You'll probably discover there is quite a difference between your best and worst runs. Consistency is what you're after and the print-out on the time slips is hard to ignore.

A day at the drags can be a fun outing for the whole family and it isn't as selfish as it might appear. There is lots of color, and if you find a classy strip, the caliber of the machinery can be outstanding. Best of all, by going out to the drags to discover the capabilities of your car, you are off the streets and placed in the only environment where speed and its quest can be conducted in relative safety—a race track.

It is on the straight where race cars make the best time and where the differences in machines are most apparent. Race drivers are consumed with a desire to straighten out the road because they know that a car performs best in a straight line. Once you've mastered the mechanics of moving along a direct course, it's time to work on the corners. So, let's see if I can give you a new line.

8
TAKING A NEW LINE

Corners come in many shapes and sizes. Learning to identify and classify them is to your benefit. Everything a driver achieves on the straight is for naught if he doesn't master the art of cornering. The first prerequisite is knowing the road. In this chapter I will discuss types of corners but not kinds. There is an important distinction. A "type" of corner is how it occurs along your path while a "kind" is the actual shape of the corner. More on that later.

Learning to read a road necessitates use of some terms that should be discussed.

Braking Point . . . That point at which the driver first applies his brakes in anticipation of a curve. Its selection is based on car speed, braking ability, distance to corner, and the driver's built-in margin for error. The braking point may be a shutoff point. In this instance, brakes are not applied but acceleration is arrested.

Entrance Point . . . The point of entry into the corner, or just as the car begins to turn into a bend.

Apex . . . The lowest, or most inside, point the car passes while negotiating a corner. An apex is an arbitrary point selected by the driver and may be located either forward or rearward of an imaginary line bisecting the radius of the corner. There may be two apexes in a corner. An apex is always located on the inside.

Radius . . . The curvature of a corner measured at the inside edge. The radius may be constant, increasing, or decreasing.

Exit Point . . . The location of the car when it resumes a straight course. Should a turn quickly follow, the exit point then becomes the subsequent turn's entrance point.

Longest Possible Radius (LPR) . . . The maximum radius that can be fitted into the road edges from entrance point to exit point. The LPR may extend past both points.

Line . . . The path described by a car passing through the entrance point, apex, and exit point. The line is the driver's selection, and he is expected to ascertain the line that is best for his car, his driving style, and the one best suited for the requirements of the corner. Rather than maintaining the same position relative to the edges of the road, the driver transcribes his own path for the following three reasons. His line may provide the shortest path, the longest radius, or the highest possible exit speed. The last is the most important reason.

This list describes the techniques and terms that a driver uses to help him with the mechanics of cornering. Understand that the act of cornering is more mechanics than anything else. No race driver in the world sets off on a track he is unfamiliar with and burns up the track. Drivers may actually walk the track before they set a wheel to turning. These scouting trips help them learn the peculiarities of the course. A driver looks for places where the pavement is broken since these spots can deprive him of a moment's traction. He checks the profile and contour of each turn to see whether there is any banking that can help him. He looks for the apex used by previous racers, checking for scuff marks on inner markers or following the "track" of rubber and oil laid down by past racers. He also looks for those places on a course where he may effectively widen the course by placing a wheel off the edge deliberately. Depressions, water flows, and other such places where water might collect attract his attention. All these matters concern him vitally. They should concern any driver interested in high-performance driving.

A well-known law in physics is that any body in motion wants to continue in a straight line relative to the direction of travel. A car at speed is a moving body. When a car is turned off a straight course the realities of centrifugal force come into being. Centrifugal force and the tire's battle with it are the limiting factors in cornering and the driver seeks ways and means to reduce the effects of centrifugal force.

The best way to reduce centrifugal force is to eliminate it entirely.

Many turns for a race driver are not turns at all because he can, by using the width of the road, drive straight through them. If he must turn, the driver seeks to lengthen the radius of the corner. The longer the radius, the higher the possible speed. The tip of a propeller travels farther than the hub but in the same amount of time so the tip speed is faster. A corner on an expressway can be taken at a higher speed than can the right-hand turn on a city street because its radius is much longer.

A road has width to accommodate one, two, three, or more lanes of traffic, and using this width effectively can increase the length of your turn. A longer radius means that the car has farther to travel but the increase in possible speed compensates for the increase in mean distance.

As you saw earlier, a car can stop more quickly than it can accelerate. Therefore, the task of the driver is to make it easier for the car to do its most difficult job, acceleration. This means that the line employed by the driver is geared toward providing him with the maximum exit speed because this speed is carried down the following straight.

The most critical moment in cornering is in the initial phase of the corner, not in the corner itself or its exit. When the moving mass (the car) is turned, the onset of centrifugal force is at its highest and most difficult to control level. Once a turn is established, the effects of inertia seek to keep the car traveling in a curved path. Since the beginning of a corner is so critical, it follows that the educated driver will lower his speed during his entrance to a corner to maximize control during the difficult period. He also assures himself a higher exit speed if he has more control and hits his apex more precisely.

The apex selection is very important. Its purpose is to achieve the highest possible exit speed, which the car reaches at the exit point. The trick is to maintain enough cornering power to negotiate the bend while accelerating. The acceleration, because it splits the tires' function, widens the arc of the car from the apex to the exit point. The outward drift, or widening arc, should end at the outside edge of the road leading away from the corner just as the turning is finished.

1. The first car has just hit the apex and is powering out, while the two cars behind are about to clip their apex. In the background, the cars have just left another turn on a very late apex to be in proper position for the foreground turn. Notice how they give themselves room for the sweep down to the corner in the foreground.

2

3

2. Oh, those awful feelings. Too much throttle in the wet. Follow his tracks.

3. Too heavy on the brakes. When you lock them up like this you cannot turn. He's looking where he wants to go.

4. The corner is finished for the lead car, Peter Revson, and behind him Mark Donohue is drifting toward the apex of the turn. Notice that the inner markers (tires buried halfway) bear the marks of the many cars literally hitting the apex. The one mashed down the most is the one most often hit. On a new course you look for things like this.

4

5

5. Number 3 has a wild-looking drift going. Number 4, behind, is getting his car set up to drop to the apex. These larger-bodied race cars have to assume larger slip angles at the rear to get around quickly.

6. The Porsche is a good example of oversteer. Its rear engine centers the weight rearward and the natural tendency is to "hang the tail out."

7. The Alfa, front-engined rear-drive, is in the midst of a low-speed turn and is understeering mightily.

6

7

8

9

8. All three men are taking the fast way through the bend, the leader coming out, the second man about to clip the apex, and the man in the background well positioned for his drop to the apex.

9. This Corvette has changed from understeer to oversteer and is well placed to brush the apex.

10. This McLaren is shown drifting right along. Notice the position of the wheels on the white line. Denny Hulme is at work.

10

11

11. This Corvette is being driven into the road by centrifugal force. Notice how the car is riding low on its suspension.

12. Porsche on the banking. Normally this Porsche would assume an over-steering attitude in a turn but the banking keeps the rear tires only slightly off line. If they tried to slide, notice that they'd have to go uphill.

13. Here's a novel approach to an apex. That inside front wheel is right on top of the course markers. He hit it this way all race long and finished third! Well, it was wet.

12

13

14. They all want the lead but they all know they have to stay on the correct line. Those are McLarens out front.

15. Downhill and to the right. Notice the rear tire of the last car in line. Number 3 is on line and still pointing to his apex, not yet on the throttle.

15

16

17

16. Same corner, different car, different line. Number 15 likes it inside.

17. Car Number 15 is consistent. Here he's a little farther into the bend and is starting his drift.

18. Oops! Number 66 is late getting into the turn.

18

19. Number 7 is taking a long shot at his apex. Compare his position to car Number 15 in photo 16.

20. Car Number 2 is going to take it inside this trip.

19

21

22

21, 22. Only the number is the same.

Since the exit speed is so important the other aspects of cornering fall into place. You know that the speed at which you enter a corner, through the first third, is not nearly as important as your speed when you exit. If you reduce speed at the entrance to a turn, you have, or at least you should have, more control and an opportunity to exploit this control by being more precise in hitting the apex and setting up the outward drift of the car under acceleration. Keep that in mind when you come to a turn you don't know and are tempted to blast through. Blast out, not in.

The maximum benefit of taking a new line comes when you can use all the road, edge to edge. You need a clear track and good visibility to do that. Swinging out into the other guy's lane to set up for that blind corner ahead may not be the worst thing you'll ever do but it may be the last.

The physical law that supports the theory of high exit speed is simple enough. If two cars come out of a turn, one at 101 mph and the other at 99 mph, and both have the same accelerative ability, the faster car has a two-mile-an-hour head start and will take less time to reach its terminal velocity and less time to cover the distance of the ensuing straight. Even on short straights this advantage can be clearly seen. If you go into a turn at a rate of speed inconsistent with control and mess up your apex and exit, you have committed a driver error. It is not necessarily the kind that results in an accident but one that raises lap times and loses races.

Examine Figure 3. The dotted line shows you the longest possible radius you can transcribe within the confines of the road edges. Hereafter I'll refer to it as LPR. The solid line shows the best path a car can take through this most common "kind" of corner if it is followed by a straight. You have seen that getting the most speed coming *out* of a turn is the primary goal of the high-performance driver. It follows that a turn that empties onto a long straight is more important, in terms of time, than a corner that is followed by yet another corner.

Primary-type turns empty onto a straight and getting through them properly, on the right line and with maximum exit speed, is more important than any other event behind the wheel. The correct pro-

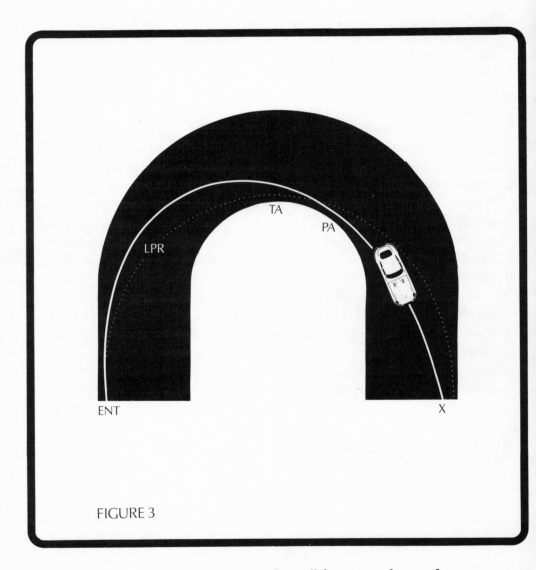

FIGURE 3

cedure in a primary-type turn can slice off fractions of seconds or even whole seconds that make all the difference in the world.

On a closed course the importance of these "types" of turns is magnified, but the approach to corner types remains the same on the street. Primary turns always occur before a straight. The longer the straight that follows a primary turn the more important that turn becomes. A race driver, in looking at a course, determines which straight is the longest and the turn that precedes it is the most important corner on the course. The next corner of importance would be the corner that empties on the second-longest straight. The driver follows this procedure until all the corners that end with a straight have been classified.

After primary turns, in terms of relative importance, come secondary turns. Secondary turns come at the end of straights. The corner at the end of the longest straight is the most important secondary turn. The build-up of speed down the long straight should be carried as far as possible if you want to lower lap times or the absolute time between points A and B. Secondary turns are also classified in a diminishing manner depending on the rate of speed the car can attain on the straight that leads into the corner.

Down the list of importance come the third-class turns, turns that are followed by another corner. Even though it looks super to watch a car dance through a series of bends, that is not where speed saves time. Much of the car's energy potential is being used to move through these corners and very little is used to increase speed. However, the last turn in the series if followed by a straight is a primary turn.

After a driver has classified all the turns into primary, secondary, and third class, he then begins the identification process, breaking each of the "types" of turns into the "kind" of corner it represents. Identifying kinds of corners involves many variables. There are constant radius, decreasing radius, two-piece, banked, off-camber, multileveled, uphill, downhill, and so on. So many, in fact, that I will devote a chapter to them and the best line through each.

Refer to Figure 3 and notice how the solid line does not follow a constant arc. The initial sweep of the turn as drawn by the car is wider in radius than the middle portion of that same line. The arc widens once the line moves past the apex. The driver has taken one constant radius corner and given it three distinct radii. By holding a car on the path of the dotted line you would move through the corner faster. But on the solid line, the last portion of the turn sees the exit arc widen so that at the end of the corner the car can attain a higher rate of speed than if the driver had stayed on the LPR because the radius of the last portion of the turn is the widest. The time lost while in the turn is made up within 40 yards of the corner, and the longer the straight, the better that advantage shows up.

Notice how the apex is located well forward of an imaginary line bisecting the turn. By moving the innermost point the car crosses, or "clips," farther forward, the exit arc has a longer radius from the apex to the exit than has the LPR.

The art of cornering depends on placement. You must be able to steer the car onto exactly the path you choose and in the smoothest manner possible. The weight shifts involved in turning the car off the straight set up a number of influences. To make sure you don't have too many imputs, here is a suggestion to help you perfect your ability to place a car.

As you drive over a winding road, check your steering wheel movements. If you have to continually monitor the wheel with a series of small corrections, you have to practice. At normal speeds you shouldn't have to do any more than turn the wheel to initiate the corner, hold it steady while you go around the turn, then unwind it when the turn is completed. Deviations from a constant path, besides setting up unnecessary inertia forces, also increase the distance traveled without a corresponding increase in speed. The entire turning process is made easier if you know the road and the exact angle of each turn.

When you are satisfied that you can place the car on any line without difficulty, try to establish a mini-line along the line as illustrated in Figure 3. Stay within the confines of your lane because it helps build discipline. On right-hand turns the left wheels should be close to the lane stripe as you set up for the corner. Midway through the corner, cross over your lane so that the right wheels are now running close to the right-side lane stripe. When you come out of the turn, you let the car track across the lane to end up with the left wheels again paralleling the left-side lane stripe. You must be proficient with this technique. It involves knowing precisely where each wheel is located and being able to place them where you want them.

In summary, centrifugal force can be reduced by increasing the effective radius of a turn. Exit speed is more important than either entrance speed or corner speed. A line (or groove) is chosen to reduce centrifugal force and gain a higher exit speed. A turn that empties onto a straight (primary) is more important than a turn at the end of a straight (secondary). A turn at the end of a straight is more important than turns that come in sequence (third class), except for the last turn in a series, which is a primary turn if a straight follows.

More than any of the above, knowing the road and its peculiarities will keep you on it.

Employing a line through a corner will allow you to achieve a higher effective turn speed. A line gives you a greater margin for error even at normal speeds. But a line gives its all when the speed is such that the car drifts. Before you make full use of a line, you have to be able to control a car that is sliding or drifting. Thus, let's move on to the next chapter, hoping that you won't mind the break in learning about corners. I'll get back to them. But first, you've got to experience and control the sensations of drifting and sliding.

9
DRIFTING AND SLIDING

The distinction between drifting and sliding is important. When a car is drifting, it is increasing speed. When a car is sliding, speed is being decreased. The perfect four-wheel drift is the dream of every driver. Some men come closer to perfection time after time and they are race drivers. In this chapter I will try to create the best circumstances for learning how to arrive at a four-wheel drift.

It is important to go back over three things that bear directly on drifting. You know that a car accelerates best when the tires are pointed straight ahead. You have seen that a tire can provide lateral resistance when it is angled off the direction of travel within a certain limit—slip angle. You have also seen that achieving a high exit speed is dependent on acceleration through a corner. Taking these three factors into account, a good driver can set up a car in such a manner as to provide side resistance for cornering, keep the wheels pointed straight ahead, and accelerate all at the same time. Ideally, you should slide into a turn and drift out.

But where can you practice drifting? It should not be done on the street. The advances in tire design require fairly high speeds to initiate any kind of slide, much less a drift. Since sliding and drifting can result in a loss of control, you must choose an area that will allow plenty of room for errors.

A parking lot makes a good skid pad, especially if it is wet or icy. You want to keep the speed down to protect against damage to pride or equipment. Make sure your skid pad is free of other cars, concrete bumpers, or light standards. Abandoned airfields also make nice skid pads but, remember, watch out for culverts or expansion cracks. They can catch on a wheel that is going sideways and put you on your head. Any flat open area with a slippery surface will do. Choose it carefully.

In Figure 4 you see the beginning of the exercise. Stake out a circle of about 200 feet in diameter. Old milk cartons make nice pylons; empty, of course. Go around this circle at low speed for a couple of times to get used to the lateral loading. Make sure you have your seat and shoulder belts done up snugly. They will keep you in place. Notice in the illustration that the front wheels are turned into the circle and the back tires are running somewhat to the inside of the track. You are about to find out how your car handles—whether it understeers or oversteers or handles neutrally. Begin to increase your speed while holding the steering wheel steady.

Understeer is shown in Figure 5; severe understeer, or "plowing," in Figure 6.

If the front end begins to slide outward and the radius of the circle gets longer, the car is understeering. This means you have to turn the wheel more to stay on your line. If, however, the speed is too great, the front end will wash out and send you to the outside.

If the rear tires begin to creep out and the circle tightens, the car is oversteering, as in Figure 7, and will require you to unwind the wheel to stay on the track. In Figure 7 you can see how to correct the "loose" tail of the oversteering car by turning into the direction of the skid. In this case the angle of the car is being held by the front tires, which are pointed sharply outward. This correction is called "opposite lock."

"Lock" describes the steering wheel that can no longer be turned, or is "locked." Lock to lock describes the full amount of travel of the steering wheel from a full left-hand turn to a full right-hand. A fast steering ratio requires far less driver effort. A slow steering ratio may go as high as six turns of the steering wheel, lock to lock. A fast steering ratio, usually three turns lock to lock or less, requires much less wheel movement for the car to answer the helm. The steering of a race car is very fast and a driver may not ever have to turn his wheel more than a half turn each way throughout the course of a race.

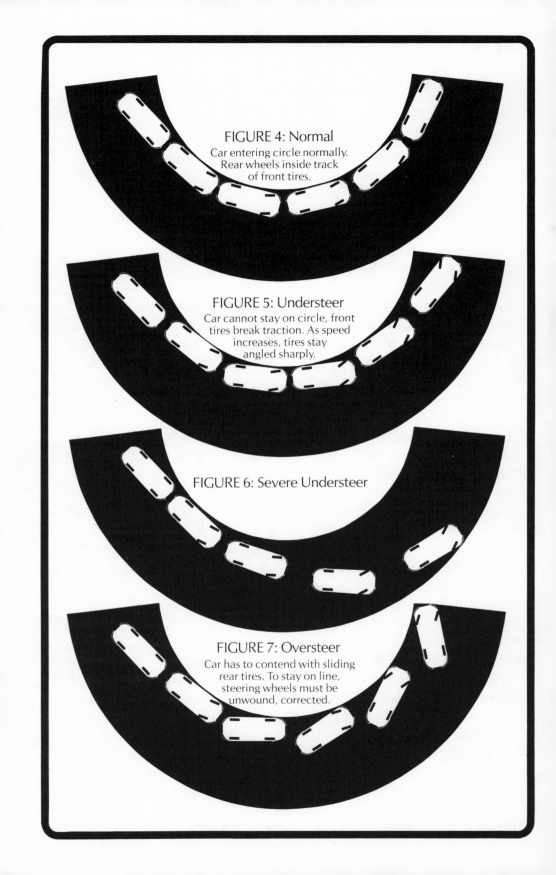

FIGURE 4: Normal
Car entering circle normally.
Rear wheels inside track
of front tires.

FIGURE 5: Understeer
Car cannot stay on circle, front
tires break traction. As speed
increases, tires stay
angled sharply.

FIGURE 6: Severe Understeer

FIGURE 7: Oversteer
Car has to contend with sliding
rear tires. To stay on line,
steering wheels must be
unwound, corrected.

A word on hand position. Try not to cross the arms when you tug the wheel around. Either slip one hand down along the wheel so you get more rotation with one movement or, if the hands have to come off the steering wheel rim, try to make the left hand end up at the nine o'clock position and the right hand at the three o'clock position when you reach a stable mode (when you no longer have to turn the wheel).

The car in Figure 7 is obviously operating past the rear tires' maximum slip angle of 10 degrees. As discussed earlier in this book, the slip angle, when exceeded, demonstrates a loss of efficiency. The front tires in this illustration are not doing much for cornering but are trying to keep the rear end of the car from passing the front.

Oversteering cars have greater slip angles at the rear tires so they always appear to be over the limit, or off line. The fastest method of getting around a corner occurs when the rear tires operate outside the line as taken by the front tires. Our next illustration shows how we can make the understeering car in Figure 5 change its attitude so its rear wheels are outside the track of the front.

Place your car on your circle again and start increasing speed. Anticipate the plowing of the front end. When the circle begins to widen, hit the throttle hard, but just for a couple of beats.

In Figure 8, the transformation from understeer to oversteer is in progress. An arrow shows the outward-sliding rear tires.

By sharply hitting the throttle, additional power is sent to the rear tires. Consequently, they have more work to do. If they start spinning, traction is reduced; and with less traction for cornering, the tires cannot hold their line so they slide outward in answer to centrifugal force. Thus, as we see in Figure 8, the rear tires creep outward. This "changeover" from understeer to oversteer can also be effected by coming off the throttle because that imparts a braking influence on the rear tires. The speed has to be fairly high to effect the changeover by lifting the throttle foot. In any case, the object is to accelerate in a corner so applying power to effect the changeover is preferable.

Figure 9 depicts what happens when you use too much power for too long to get into the oversteering attitude. This also occurs if you

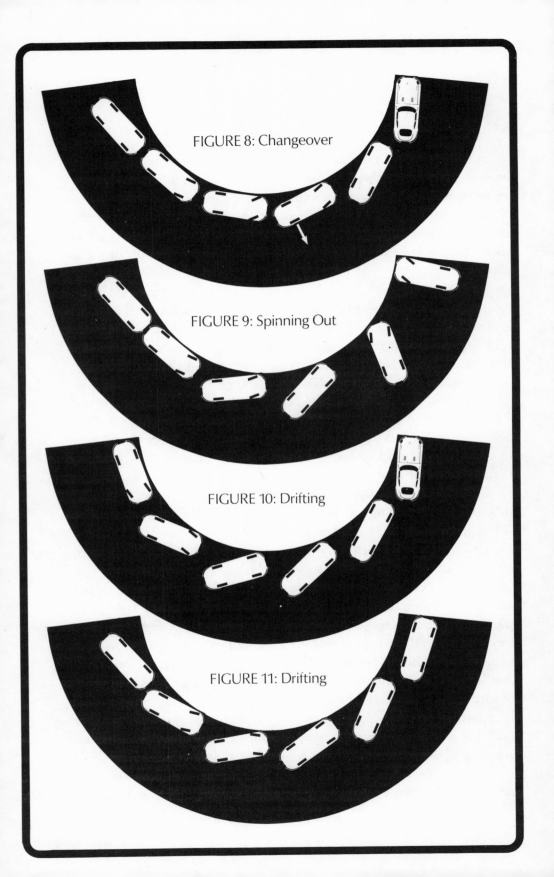

FIGURE 8: Changeover

FIGURE 9: Spinning Out

FIGURE 10: Drifting

FIGURE 11: Drifting

don't put in enough opposite lock, or correction, fast enough. It is the classic spin. At low speeds, spins will send you toward the inside of the turn. At high speeds, you spin to the outside. These are not hard-and-fast rules. Speed is being lost while in a spin and the car's attitude toward the direction of travel is also changed. That means that a car can do some strange things while spinning. If you are behind a car that goes into a spin, the best place to head is right at him. He won't be there when you arrive . . . maybe.

In a front-wheel-drive car, understeer is very decided. Hitting the throttle when the circle is widening only makes the front tires (which are receiving power) work harder and lateral resistance suffers. Lifting your throttle foot in a front-wheel-drive car tends to make the car head to the inside of the corner.

Figure 10 shows what the car and wheels look like when all the forces acting on it are in equilibrium, or balance. The car, as illustrated, is holding its line. Power is being applied to the rear wheels while the front wheels are pointed straight ahead. The turning is accomplished by the car's attitude. The rear wheels want to drive the car inward but the speed is such that the car also wants to slide outward. All four tires are slipping slightly yet not so much that they aren't doing their job.

Getting into this attitude requires practice. A basically under-steering car is perhaps easiest to hold in this posture. An oversteering car gets into this attitude much easier, however, since this is its natural tendency. In both cases, judicious use of the throttle in conjunction with adept steering wheel control can hold this posture long enough to get through any corner. Because a drift calls for acceleration you cannot hold like this forever. Eventually the speed forces you outward, as in Figure 11. It is this outward drift that takes you to the exit point of a corner. As you pass the exit point, all side forces should cease and the car is then free to bomb down the straight.

Learning to catch and then hold a slide also requires practice. By keeping your hands on the three and nine o'clock position on the steering wheel you'll find it far easier to know just how much you have turned or how much correction you have cranked in.

The initial steering influence often determines how much correction you have to add. Inertia is at work here. If you turn sharply to initiate a turn, the car's reaction will also occur sharply. Centrifugal force sets in suddenly, and the weight of the car, acting through the center of gravity, shifts to the outside tires. This brings the entire car, from rims to roof, outside the path as taken by the treads. The tires and suspension now have to react to the sudden onslaught of lateral force, first to stop the weight shift, then to hold it. As in braking, the suddenness is what causes the problems. The shifting weight sets up its own inertia and it does not want to stop. In order to regain balance you hurriedly have to put in more correction than you would like.

A slide can only be initiated by speed, turning the steering wheel too far too fast, or braking and turning. Since the object is to slide into a turn and drift out, you should now practice setting up these slides.

Take a straight running start toward your circle at a speed just above that which you have already discovered will allow you to hold the line. When you reach your circle, turn the wheel sharply. As soon as centrifugal force sets in, lift your throttle foot. The rear tires should start to slide. If the front tires plow, your speed of entry was too high. Try again. Some plowing can be anticipated, but if your speed is correct, the front tires will slide for a moment then catch hold. As soon as you feel the rear tires tracking outward, get back on the throttle. You don't want to add power yet. Just take up the slack with a feathered throttle to hold your speed. This starts the weight moving to the rear and allows the car to establish its balance. From this point it is easier to add power to set up a drifting posture.

Another method of setting up the initial slide, or to change understeer to oversteer, is to brake as you start onto your circle. We know that tires will not perform as well when they have to deal with two influences so modulate your braking effort as you begin to turn. In this exercise, approach at a speed that will require braking and resist braking until the last possible moment. As you turn, take some pressure off the brake pedal. If you don't, the wheels will be very prone to lock up.

The front tires in braking have more weight on them so the rear tires (with less weight and traction) should track outward quite easily.

If the speed is correct when you enter the circle, you will begin to slide. In anticipation of this slide, be ready to unwind the steering wheel and imput opposite-lock correction. When the slide is in progress, come off the brake and get your right foot on the throttle. The weight shifts rearward and should give the rear tires more bite which, in turn, should end the slide and establish balance. Two problems crop up when you use the brakes to start a slide. First, you may brake too late, which results in an entry speed that is too high. Second, when you brake as you turn, the wheels may lock. If that happens, all control will be lost until you come off the brakes.

Learn to approach a corner smoothly. Radical movements of the steering wheel are unnecessary except in low-speed (first gear) corners. Hairpin corners (switchbacks) require very sharp angles up front and the steering wheel sometimes really has to be cranked around. In any case, you want to enter a turn at a speed that causes the car to start sliding in a controlled fashion. You want to effect the changeover as quickly and as smoothly as possible. An oversteering car adopts this changeover naturally. The understeering car will change over in any one of three ways: application of power, reduction in power, as in lifting off the throttle, or by braking and turning at the same time. Practice putting a car into a slide.

Bear in mind that both ends are connected, and if you lose one end, both are going off the road.

Many of our fears about driving exist because we've never been there before. Once you become accustomed to drifting and sliding you will lose your fear of them. Pay close attention to those feelings that are transmitted to you from the steering wheel. You will be able to feel the bite of the tires through the amount of strength it takes to turn or hold the wheel. The most news will come to you through the "seat of your pants."

You must be able to select in advance the spot where you want to effect the changeover from slide to drift or understeer to oversteer. Place a small pylon halfway around the circumference of your circle to practice this. Try to come as close to it as possible with your inside front tire when you drift under acceleration. Use the pylon as your apex and "clip" it. Use it as your entrance point. Use the pylon as your exit point. Force yourself into this selection. Neither a slide nor a drift is of any value if it doesn't occur at your command. You can only discover the methods through practice.

Guessing at the performance of your car or trying to divine its properties without actually testing yourself and the car is stupidity. Making such a test in the wrong place at the wrong time is also stupidity. There is no reason to find out about your car at 100 mph on smooth concrete when the same things can be learned at 20 mph on ice. The car's behavior will be exactly the same, but the speed is obviously safer. Find a spot with a consistent, slippery surface. You'll learn more about yourself and your car in an hour on a skid pad than you'd learn from a month of practice on the street. You see the sense in that, I'm sure.

Let's review our progress to this point. Braking and acceleration are optimized in a straight line. Exit speed is more important than entrance speed or absolute cornering speed. The function of the line you take through a corner is to lengthen its radius for a higher turn and exit speed. The apex is the most important part of any corner since it sets up your exit arc. Getting to the next corner is dependent on the speed with which you exit the previous one. There are three "types" of turns, and if you miss one, you miss them all. There is a difference between drifting and sliding. Weight is a function of traction and it can shift on a chassis. A tire performs best when its optimum slip angle is not exceeded.

Now let's put into practice what has been learned on the skid pad.

10
GETTING AROUND

This chapter brings the techniques, skills, and conditions together. Each kind of corner will be discussed—first, its location on the road; second, its highest potential; and last, its highest exit speed.

Let's assume that the track is perfectly clear, unshared by man or beast, and that the surface gives consistent traction. The "lines" as illustrated will use all the road and are meant only as a guide, for every corner has its own little quirks and only practice can show you the quickest way through them.

Setting up for a turn, both mentally and physically, requires concentration and attention to every sense. The most difficult part of cornering is the first phase of every corner (entry), where either through lack of concentration or misreading, a driver finds himself in trouble. Depth perception has a lot to do with this.

Depth perception relates directly to closing rates. Because we have two eyes we are able, some better than others, to judge how far things are from us and how fast we or they are approaching. In the case of an automobile at speed, proficiency at judging closing rates relates directly to how soon you have to brake for a turn and how much time you have to effect a pass. It is also part and parcel of crossing a highway or joining the fray on an expressway. Practicing your depth perception can take place any time you get behind the wheel and the speed really isn't important. Practice with the mirrors as well.

Try to determine just how soon and at what point you will pass the car coming at you in the other lane. When approaching a turn, pick out a spot in advance as your braking point and judge your performance. In this way you can gradually close up the slack until you are able, through feel, familiarity, and experience, to gauge your speed and the space needed to reach the proper entrance speed. On a freeway, try to determine your closing rate over other cars. Make a game of locating all the cars you can see and figuring out where they will be in five seconds.

Race drivers have two outstanding skills. One is their ability to continue to react in surprise situations. The other is their vision, of which depth perception is a large part. Knowing closing rates is especially important in having the right speed for a turn. In most corners your braking should be finished just as you begin to turn the steering wheel. In secondary-type turns you brake into the turn itself.

Going "deep" into a turn, a driver carries his speed a little farther, the brakes being applied right into the first portion of the corner rather than completing all braking before the turn. The importance of knowing your closing rate is clearly evident when you go in "deep." If you have too much speed when you go deep you will have a problem. It isn't as bad if you err on the side of caution. The late-braking approach makes it very easy to start a slide, as you know from your time spent on the skid pad.

In front-wheel-drive vehicles this late-braking approach has considerably more value since it is difficult to get a front-wheel-drive car to alter its posture for maximum turn speed. By using the deep approach, you can get the lightly loaded rear end to come out for you, then catch it with the throttle as you continue around the turn. When you hit the throttle, just as in rear-wheel-drive cars, the weight shifts aft and the sliding rear tires pick up more traction.

You don't always plan on late braking but may find yourself in the unenviable position of needing that little extra room to get your speed down so you can make it around the corner. If you know that the car can be set up with the brakes, it will keep you from panicking when you have misjudged the closing rate and your braking distance, or if your brakes start to fade. Modulate your brake pressure as you begin the turn and you'll probably be surprised that you can make it around. A car can take off a lot of speed in a very short distance; usually, just enough to keep you on the road. Cars used to behave very strangely when you applied the brakes and attempted to turn but cars today have pretty good manners.

It is very important that you be totally familiar with each corner on your path. Speed around a turn should not come right away but should build up to its maximum. A car's behavior can change radically as speed builds up, and by limiting yourself to gradual increases in speed you won't be surprised. Also, by gradually increasing your speed you will be able to make the modifications to your line as best suit the particular corner you are tackling.

The most common corner is the constant radius turn. The length of the radius (measured at the inside edge) remains constant from the moment the curve begins until it ends.

The theoretical maximum turn speed would occur when the car transcribed the path as shown by the dotted line in Figure 12, since that is the longest possible radius that you can fit into the edges of the road. The innermost point along the dotted line is the theoretical apex. The dotted line provides no room for acceleration but would, if followed, take the car from the entrance to the exit in the shortest amount of time. That, however, is not the fastest way to the *next* corner which lies down the succeeding straight. If you come into this turn at top speed and cannot increase speed or if you come into it at a very low speed (say a very slow corner came just before) and could assume full acceleration all the way through, you would then follow the LPR.

The object, as I've discussed, is to pass the exit point at the highest possible rate of speed since that speed is then carried down the succeeding straight. To accomplish this you trace your line through the corner as shown by the solid line in Figure 12. By moving the practical apex forward of the theoretical apex you have successfully lengthened the exit arc of the corner (from practical apex to exit) and this increase allows for maximum accelerative values which will, because the radius is longer, allow you to pass the exit point at a higher rate of speed. The solid line shows the correct line for a constant radius turn of the primary type.

By starting into the corner from the left-hand edge of the road, you have lengthened the radius by the width of the road. That trans-

LPR

A

FIGURE 12

lates into a higher initial cornering speed. From the entrance point to the apex, however, because you are following the solid line and not the LPR, you are heading to the inside of the corner and your radius

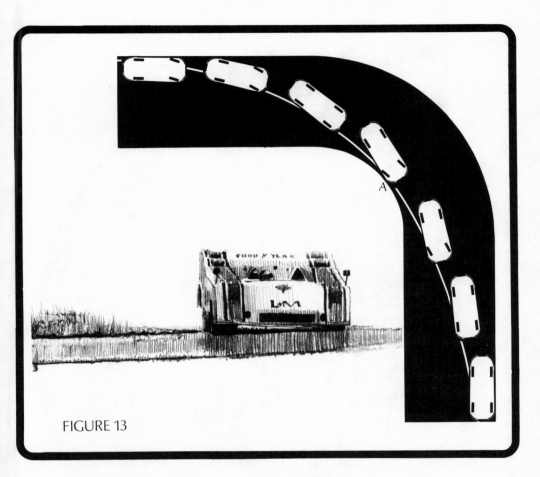

FIGURE 13

is now shorter than the LPR, which means less speed. This loss is made up by the increasing nature of the exit arc, which from the apex on is longer than the LPR and allows more speed. Whether this corner can be taken at 100 mph or 50 mph, the line, as illustrated, would be the correct one so long as the corner is followed by a straight.

If the corner came up after a straight and lets out onto another straight, as in Figure 13, you would be tempted to treat it as a secondary-type corner. Whenever there is a choice between secondary and primary, make it a practice to treat the corner as a primary-type turn. If a corner quickly followed the corner in Figures 12 and 13, you would then treat Figures 12 and 13 as secondary corners, as shown in the next illustration.

FIGURE 14

Figure 14 illustrates another constant radius turn but the line is for a late-braking approach with an early apex that swings wide, then on to a second apex.

Make no mistake, improper use of the brakes here can place you sideways very easily and ruin the traction of the tires, which are working hard to combat centrifugal force. The feeling can make you very queasy because the car feels as though it were on ice. When you think of it, it is no worse than the same feeling you get when the car is drifting. In both cases the car is busy doing two things at once (braking and turning or accelerating and turning) and doing both less efficiently. But the blending or consolidation is what results in higher speeds.

In Figure 14, the approach curve to the early apex starts farther back on the prior straight than it does in Figures 12 and 13. This gives a smooth long-radiused approach to the corner, which carries the speed much farther along. The changeover point (when you get off the brakes and onto the throttle to catch your slide) must be carefully chosen. Here's where the importance of being able to cause a slide when you want it comes in. As soon as you effect the changeover, head the car to a very late apex. Remember, this approach is worthwhile only when another corner quickly follows and you have no room to accelerate. In Figure 14 you have created two apexes, with the first being the most important in terms of time as the speed you have built up down the prior straight is carried "deep" into the turn.

As third-class turns, Figures 12, 13 and 14 would be taken on the LPR. Remember to draw your LPR so that the exit point becomes your entrance point to the next corner, and if that entrance point requires you to be in the middle of the road for the best approach to the next turn, that is where your own version of the LPR should end. When turns come in sequence the proper placement of the car for the next turn is very important. Each exit then becomes the entrance to the next curve and so on until the last turn in the series occurs. The last turn is a primary corner and you must place your car for the most advantageous line through the last turn. Always try to think one corner ahead.

An understeering car will require more steering effort to initiate the line, while an oversteering car may do it all too quickly. Make allowances for your car's natural tendencies. Once you have started on your line, choose a throttle opening that maintains the speed of the car through the first phase of the drop down to the apex or slightly increase your speed until at the apex you accelerate as much as conditions permit. Beware of sudden movements of the steering wheel or throttle. Concentrate on smoothness. It isn't hard to put a car off the road, even at speeds well below maximum potential.

In the beginning it is best to practice on a low-speed constant radius turn. Start out slowly and make sure you know exactly where you want the car in relation to the road edges. Then, gradually build up speed to a point that places the rear tires outside of the front tires as early in the turn as possible. Remember that the slip angle should not exceed 15 degrees for bias tires or 10 degrees for radials. The front tires should not be turned too far in the first phase of the corner nor should you have to imput a lot of opposite-lock correction once the car assumes its drift.

In cars with little power or at speeds where hard acceleration is not possible, move the apex back closer to the theoretical apex. If you have a lot of power on tap, the apex should be moved even farther forward than shown in Figures 12 and 13 since the car will drift out farther when you have it in a drift.

Many cars that understeer naturally at low speeds will adopt an oversteering tendency at higher speeds. This occurs because the power that is being fed into the tires to maintain speed is already taking up a large portion of the tire's total available traction. This doesn't apply to front-wheel-drive machines.

You want to get the weight heeled over and stabilized as quickly as possible so the suspension doesn't have to deal with shifting weight. Weight shifts will occur with every movement of the steering wheel or throttle. No road gives consistent traction so there will be some corrections necessary. Just try to make as few as possible.

The entrance to a curve is most critical but the apex is the most important point on any turn. That is where you want to go when you begin the corner, and the more positive you are when you first commit to a line, the easier it will be to get there. If you hit an apex that is too early, your increasing arc may run you out of road. If you hit the apex too late or too far around the turn, you won't hit the exit point at the highest rate of speed. If you don't get the car all the way down to the apex (running wide), watch out for hard acceleration because missing an apex by 2 feet may translate into 10 feet when you get to the exit point and that 10 feet might lie off the tarmac.

Since an increasing, or expanding, radius is precisely what you want when powering out of a turn, the corner in Figure 15 lends itself to speed. If you get out of shape early during the entrance you lose the benefit built into the corner. The dotted line shows the theoretical line of the LPR. The solid line shows the line that will result in the highest exit speed.

If Figure 15 came at the end of a long straight (secondary), you would carry your speed into the turn as far as possible by using the late-braking approach. By its nature, however, an increasing radius allows for a long period of acceleration, which means time saved, and rather than risk losing the turn's advantage, it would be best to come into the turn at a controlled rate with all braking finished to make sure you have the correct line for the exit arc. Notice that the apex occurs early in this kind of bend.

Many turns come in sequence and go in the same direction, as in Figure 16, so that the exit sweep from the first of the series leads directly into the entrance of the second. The turns at Indianapolis fall into the two-piece category now that the speeds are so high.

The dotted line shows the longest possible radius through both turns in a continuing loop. The first portion of the turn is marked A, the second B. The object is to get through the second part with the highest possible exit velocity. You have a couple of options.

As illustrated, this first way of getting through involves staying outside to trace the longest possible radius that will still allow for an expanding exit arc. The apex in B is very late. Here, the line to the apex in B is started just as turn A is left behind. The timing on two-piece turns is critical. If you get inside too early in A, you will be out of position for the late apex in B, by far the most important portion of

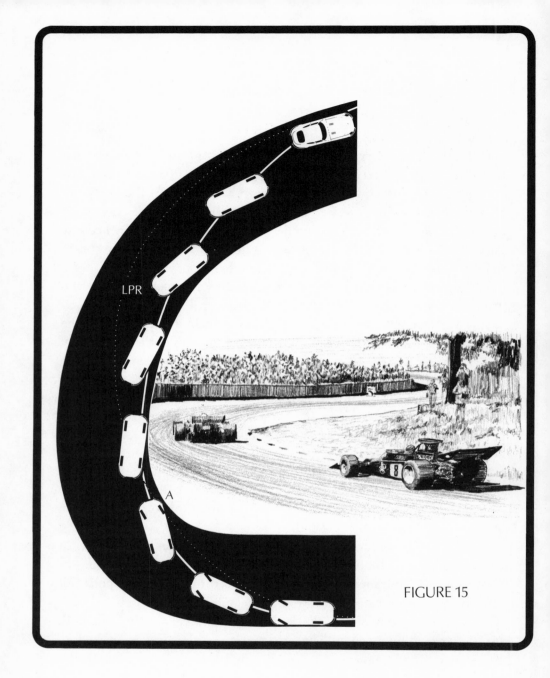

LPR

A

FIGURE 15

the turn. If your speed between the two turns doesn't keep you outside, you'll enter B on a line that will clip an early apex and the exit from B will be slowed.

Another method of going through a two-piece turn of the shape illustrated is to catch an early apex in A that will allow you to sweep wide between corners then pull down to a late apex in B, almost on

LPR

A

FIGURE 16

the path of the LPR. This route may feel better, if only because you are inside and have a lot of road to work with.

There is also the late-braking approach that uses an early apex in A, lets the arc of the sliding car move outward in preparation for the late apex in B, and picks up time at both ends of the turn. If you enter this turn by means of a straight, this line may be best since your speed is carried well into the turn.

As in all turns that come in sequence, it's the last bend that is most important. In planning a line for a two-piece turn try treating the second turn (B) as you would if it stood alone on your path. Start from the middle of the short connecting straight and plan your best line through B, then plot a course through A that will deposit you precisely on the optimum entrance point for B.

A decreasing radius turn, shown in Figure 17, is the most dangerous turn you will face. If you know the road, this turn won't jump out at you. It is no fun at all to think you have a turn wired and then find it tightening up on you.

Entering the corner from a straight, stay way outside until you drop down to a very late apex. A decreasing radius turn is working against you all the way so you have to take extra precautions. If you start into this corner too early, chances are you'll slide off to the outside. The problem is magnified if you get on the accelerator too early. Hold off as long as you can before you set the car's balance with the throttle. An understeering car will give you fits on this kind of corner.

Some decreasing radius turns permit the use of the brakes through them but you have to be able to control a brake-induced slide to get the benefits of this approach. Generally you'll find yourself on a trailing throttle through the first portion of the turn with your mind wondering when the curve is going to end. Decreasing radius turns are the hardest to get through and require patience and practice.

Two areas, especially, present problems. First, there is a great danger of misreading the corner and setting up for it as if it were a constant radius corner. That leads to an apex that comes too early. Secondly, hard acceleration coming out of a decreasing radius turn can find you with no more road with which to work. If you know one is coming, stay outside and plan on a very late apex.

Esses, or chicanes, are third-class corners. The last turn is the most important. An open ess, as in Figure 18, can be taken on your line of

LPR

A

FIGURE 17

FIGURE 18

sight with hardly a wrinkle. Remember that the side-to-side forces in going through a series of corners that quickly follow one another can upset the balance of your car. Don't try to force a car through esses. If your car has good transient response characteristics, try to establish a rhythm while you go through. Smoothness will result in better speed.

FIGURE 19

A¹

A²

In Figures 19 and 20 (closed esses) the rules call for having your car at the point that will give you the line that will result in the highest exit speed for the last corner in the series. Notice that the final corner, even though of the same radius, has a much longer effective radius than the initial curve. Esses should be taken with as little slip angle as

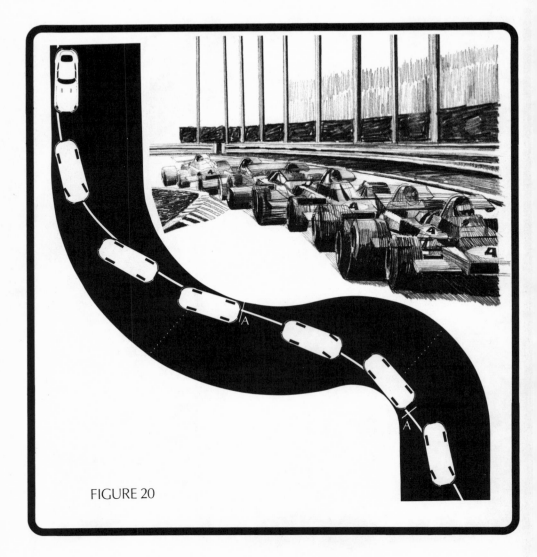

FIGURE 20

possible. If you get sideways anywhere along the way you are losing time and are probably going to miss the next bend.

Esses generally call for a steady rate of speed. In practicing, build up to your speed gradually. Don't try to pick the full speed out of the hat. You may find that one of the turns in the sequence is a lot tighter than you thought.

If one turn in the series requires braking, plan an approach that will give you as straight a line as possible for braking. Even if you

FIGURE 21

aren't using the whole road, edge to edge, just by using all of your lane you can raise your average speed through esses.

Remember that the suspension is squashed down when you track through a corner, and bumps, potholes, expansion cracks, and drainage channels will jostle your car to the outside of any turn. If you encounter a stone or water while going through a turn, don't try to horse the car to the inside (unless there is no place else to go) because it's easier to widen your arc than it is to tighten it up.

The inside portions of turns may have broken paving and when you come across sections of pavement that reduce your traction, even though they are on the correct line, be ready with an alternate line. The outside portions of turns are usually slippery, with all the small stones, dirt, and other debris kicked out there by other cars. Remember that centrifugal force is the enemy and the only thing that fights your battle for you is the tires and a poor surface doesn't help a bit. If you have to modify your line, do so.

It would serve no further purpose to list all the variables that can crop up with corners. Each is a world to itself. If you classify the relative importance of the turn (type), then properly identify its kind, you will have a handy reference system that facilitates learning the road. How does the corner occur on your path? Can you pick up time on it? Answer these questions and you've taken a huge step in learning to control your car and even more important, yourself.

The contour of the road plays a large part in determining the correct speed for any turn. In the next chapter I'll run down the contour changes to look for.

11
SHAPE OF THINGS TO COME

Corners are not the only variation from the straight and smooth. There are what some drivers call "vertical curves," by which they mean humps, hollows, dips, or flyovers.

There are also banked and off-camber slopes, in addition to uphill and downhill sections. These changes in height can be used to your advantage in driving. If you know how the shape, or contour, of the road will affect your car, you'll avoid the results of misreading the road.

As you can see in Figure 22, uphill sections produce shorter braking distances because the car is, in effect, being driven into the hill. The car, like any moving mass, wants to go straight; and when the brakes are applied, the weight shifts forward toward a point under the road, either far ahead of the car if the slope is not steep or closer to the front bumper if the road's inclination is pronounced.

Uphill turns can be taken at a faster speed than if the same turns were on the flat. You have seen that a car will go through a corner much faster if the rear tires are running outside the track of the front tires. Going uphill in a drifting posture, rear wheels outside the front, you have more traction because the car is drifting *into* the slope. The inclination holds the rear end of the car in position since to pass the front end the rear tires would have to slide uphill.

You can accelerate going downhill in a more spirited fashion, but when it comes time to slow, your braking distances are increased. The weight shifts that occur in braking cannot place as much weight on the front tires and the car's inertia carries it forward. The direction of

FIGURE 22

the forces at work while going downhill have been exaggerated in Figure 23 to give you a better idea of their direction.

Going around a downhill corner can make control ticklish. The car has a very light feeling which is caused by the car moving down the fall line of the slope. When you achieve a drifting posture, rear wheels outside the track of the front, the natural tendency of the car is to swap ends.

Treat downhill corners with respect! It's very easy to be lulled into a false sense of security. There are three points to be concerned about. First, your braking distances will be increased. Second, the changeover from sliding to drifting will occur more rapidly since the centrifugal force is being aided by the fall line of the road. Third, the exit arc, which widens naturally under acceleration, is easily underestimated, and can result in running out of road.

Banked corners, like uphill slopes, provide increased weight, as shown by the line of centrifugal force in Figure 24. Few of us will ever find ourselves on the severe banking that is found on super tracks like Daytona. But some banking is present in almost every corner you'll ever come across. Even a banking of 3 degrees can make a profound difference in cornering speed, all of it to your advantage.

Since weight is being added to the car as it presses itself against the road, the time necessary to build up speed is increased because it takes more power to move a heavier object. It also takes more energy to set up a drift, so your throttle opening will increase. The added weight means the suspension is being compressed, and small ridges in the road, which your car would normally handle with ease, are liable to upset the tires' relationship with the road. All in all, when centrifugal force glues your car to a banked road, the security feels tremendous.

If a road can be banked in your favor it can be banked to your

FIGURE 23

FIGURE 24

disadvantage as well. This type of slope is called off-camber and is illustrated in Figure 25. It is the exact opposite of a banked corner. Off-camber surfaces make the car work very hard to stay on the road. You get a very queer feeling when you go around an off-camber corner because nothing seems to work right. It is much like a downhill turn in that the rear tires will readily track outward to creep down the slope. There aren't many off-camber bends, but when they crop up, you must be cautious.

Here, centrifugal force has the upper hand because the line of

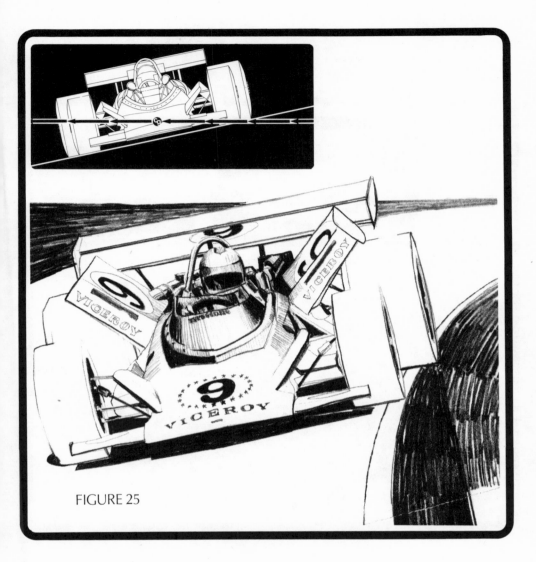

FIGURE 25

force, as shown acting through the center of gravity, leaves the road rather than pressing you and the car into it. In off-camber corners, the car loses weight and that detracts from the total available traction. As in downhill corners, several areas merit special attention. Your braking distances will not be affected but your initial steering imput will have a tendency to feel sluggish as the car has to turn up the slope from an odd angle. Also, your track, or line, which should carry you inward to the apex, is also uphill and the car won't feel like it is going to make it even though the rear wheels begin to slide out easily. And finally,

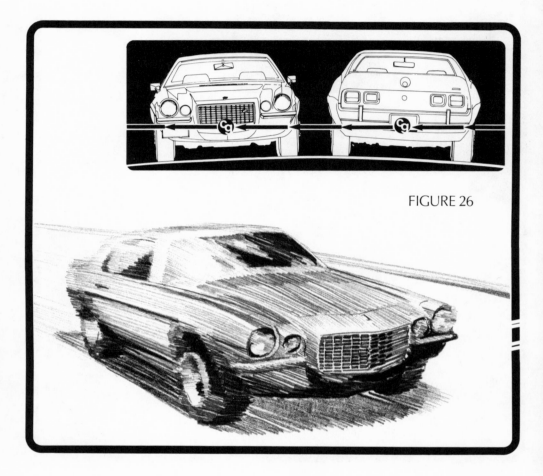

FIGURE 26

hard acceleration in coming out of an off-camber turn must be han-
dled carefully as the widening arc takes you down the fall line of the
curve and that may leave you with no more road.

A crowned road, as shown in Figure 26, can be found on those
country trails that we all like. You can readily see why it is called a
"crowned road." Notice that you have two types of banking within the
boundaries of one road. Crowned roads are built to accommodate
drainage and are usually accompanied by ditches on either side, which
can make going off a deadly affair.

If the road goes to the right, you'll want to be on the banked, or right-hand, side of the road to take advantage of the effects of banking. If the road goes to the left, the opposite side is where you want to be. Remember, however, that the left side is the other guy's lane. If someone is coming the other way, you are forced to stay on your side (the right) and then the corner to the left becomes an off-camber curve with all the attendant problems.

In plotting a line through a corner you want to be able to use all of the road from edge to edge. On highways, or any public road, for that matter, using all the road is not only dangerous, it is unlawful. Your sense of responsibility and judgment has to be the guide. If you are using all the road, there are certain difficulties you should be prepared for on a crowned road. They come when you cross over from one side of the road and its slope to the other side.

This "crossover," coming from the off-camber side to the banked, or vice versa, creates problems in the first phase of the corner, when the car has to climb the slope to the crest before it heads down the banking to the apex, and during the exit arc, when you cross over from the banked slope to the off-camber side under acceleration. If you remember to make allowances for the car's tendency to let the rear wheels outward more quickly on the off-camber side during the entry phase to the corner, you will be able to hold its attitude when the crossover is completed. When, under acceleration, you exit the turn, your widening arc will carry you back over the crest and this exit crossover must be anticipated. Once the car is on the off-camber side, the exit arc, because you are in effect going downhill, will swing out farther still.

The slope of crowned roads is seldom as severe as depicted in the illustration. Just a slight inclination makes a difference, however, and particularly on the exit crossover, the 3 feet you may add to your exit arc can be enough to create havoc.

Staying on your own side of the road is the lawful thing to do, of course. In doing so, keep in mind that there is a slight speed difference between left- and right-hand turns on a crowned road with the advantage going to the latter.

The slope change on a crowned road is but one type of crossover.

There are four others that the driver at speed must be aware of. The first occurs when a corner starts out as an uphill curve and then flattens out within the radius of the corner. The second occurs when you are heading downhill into a corner and the road flattens out. The third and fourth are when the road starts out flat and then drops downhill or sweeps uphill.

Multileveled corners are not rare and understanding how the forces will cause the car to behave can help you stay on the road.

The two multileveled corners that give some advantage to the driver are the corner that starts out flat and then swoops uphill and the corner that begins downhill and then flattens out. In both cases the car's inertia drives the car into the road's surface.

The time lost on the entrance to the downhill curve that flattens out can be made up as soon as the car crosses the slope change. At that point, the car, which has been traveling downward, is pressed into the road and traction is increased. When a corner starts out flat and then goes uphill the driver can make use of the inertia that is forcing the car into the road, which means increased traction, by getting on the throttle earlier and harder. In both cases a later apex is called for.

The two multileveled corners that give the driver problems are a corner that begins as an uphill bend but flattens out and a corner that begins as flat as a table and then falls downward. In both of these cases, when the car hits the crossover, inertia causes the body to lift, which takes weight off the tires and traction is therefore reduced. If the slope change is severe, as it can be, the driver must beware. It's no fun when you sail around a turn to have the bottom drop out on you. The car feels and acts as though it were floating. If you are trying to manage a drift or slide when it happens, control can be difficult.

These two slope changes will exaggerate the natural tendencies of your car. If your car understeers, the front end may wash out. If your car oversteers, the rear may come right around the front. The side-to-side and pitching motion set up by slope changes can give you a busy time at the wheel. If you're prepared, however, and that means knowing the road, it's relatively easy to deal with these crossovers.

In an uphill-to-flat corner, use the upward slope for your braking and turning approach if the bend is a secondary type, or to effect a more exaggerated entrance curve. What you want to do is get most of the turning out of the way before the slope change sneaks up on you. Then, when the bottom drops out, use the reduced traction to assume your drifting posture. Your line, then, would start toward the apex much sooner with a shorter radius (less speed). Once the car settles (which you can help with a little throttle), you continue around on your normal line.

In a flat-to-downhill corner you again try to get as much turning out of the way as possible. When you pass the crossover point, the car will move outward and leave you on what would, if the corner were flat, be your normal line.

Crossovers can pop up in the beginning phases of a turn, in the middle of the corner, or at the end. If the slope change occurs at the beginning, start your turn earlier. If during the middle, make your initial curve a bit tighter, which means less speed. If it occurs at the end, move your apex well forward and take precautions on your exit arc.

Professional drivers use changes in contour to their advantage, playing the slope changes to induce slides or drifts when the car is light and getting the most out of their machines in braking, acceleration and turning when the car feels heavy.

Sometimes a road provides a surprise that is hard to deal with. It's the slope change that gets you airborne. Another is that dip someone forgot to warn you about. Both can be dangerous.

The hardest part of being in the air is the landing. It is brutal on tires and suspension. When you are in the air you have absolutely no control over the car. If you are the least bit sideways when you launch, you'll come down in an awkward position. Even if you aren't sideways, the car will pitch violently when it lands and it takes some time for the car to reassert its stability.

Hitting a flyover under hard braking is not a good idea. When you are braking, the front suspension is compressed with the added weight; and when the hump throws you in the air, the suspension releases its energy, making matters worse instead of better. Also, most drivers tend to leave their foot on the brake pedal while in the air and that means that the wheels, which are weightless, lock up, and as soon as you hit, you're skidding, a very dangerous situation. Braking will tend to slam the front end of the car into the road as well. You'll do better if you get all your braking done before the front wheels leave the ground. Whatever speed you are able to take off will lessen the distance and the landing shock.

If you see you are going to be airborne, try to have the car pointed as straight as possible. Be sure your foot isn't on the gas pedal either. Without the weight of the car, the rear tires spin fearfully, which can result in overrevving the engine. Or even worse, when the car lands and the rear tires crunch down, the wheelspin will set up additional problems.

There are two tricks that can be used on flyovers, one for when you *think* you're going to take off, the other when you *know* you are. In the maybe situations, tap the brakes as the front wheels start over the hump. This pulls the nose down and may keep the tires on the road. When a flight is in the making, however, give the throttle a stiff jolt as the front wheels cross over. The brief moment of acceleration lifts the nose and can lessen the force of impact. On really long flights nothing helps. You can expect to find yourself buried, nose first, in the concrete.

Dips, those bone-jarring, eyeball-jittering thumps you always seem to encounter, can also put a car out of control. As in a flyover, try to have the car pointed straight ahead. This way, the car will have to deal only with the fore-and-aft pitching and not the dangerous side-to-side forces that can set up fishtailing. If you brake over a dip, you have limited the suspension's travel and that results in a worse situation. Get your braking, what little there may be left to you, accomplished before you hit the hollow. Don't attempt to stand on the brakes while the car is pitching. There is a real danger of getting out of control since the wheels alternately have more, then less weight on them. Hold the wheel straight and ride it out.

Some dips are worse at low speeds than when you are really moving. At faster speeds the tires don't have time to react to the dip and may, if the other side of the hollow is lower or if the dip is narrow, just step right over without ever dropping into the depression. Just remember that a dip can play havoc with the undercarriage. Control suffers when the front suspension collapses and leaves you sliding along on your belly.

By now you have a working knowledge of how to "read" a road. Hopefully you will use this knowledge to first learn a road. Concentrate on classifying corners, identifying their kind, and don't forget to take their contour into account. You might come across a multileveled, off-camber, decreasing radius primary corner with a flyover at its entrance and it's nice to know what to call it.

12
TOURING

Practice. It's the only way to learn. Automobiles are a part of our daily lives and that makes practice a breeze. Good driving techniques have less to do with speed than generally supposed so you can practice and hone the art of driving even on that run to the market. In fact, day-to-day driving forms more concrete driving patterns than handling a car on a race track. Most people are concerned about the destination, not the journey, and in this way they allow themselves to fall into bad driving habits that are hard to break. If you concentrate in everyday driving, always beginning with buckling up, you can quickly ingrain a new routine.

From the first moment, you must realize that there are two kinds of driving situations, urban and rural; and with each, a different style of driving should be brought into play. In an urban environment you are operating in a controlled and confining setting that should and reasonably does restrict the full use of the performance abilities of the automobile. In rural environments, with less congestion, the driver and his attitude become the limiting factors in the sensible use of a car.

Automobiles are the most advanced form of rapid transit yet devised, and as a part of that system you are responsible, and even obligated, in part, for its function. In city driving you must avoid maneuvers that threaten another driver.

You almost have to view city driving as you would classifying corners. Can you save time? Usually the answer is no and good sense dictates joining rather than fighting. There are a number of logical patterns to follow in urban battles. Lights, for example, are generally timed and it doesn't make sense to beat what cannot be beaten. Driving at a steady 32 mph and hitting all the lights is far safer than rushing off the line at an intersection only to arrive at the next light too early for its sequence.

The defensive-driving school of thought has received wide publicity and its basic tenets are excellent, especially in urban motoring. "Watching out for the other guy" ought to influence all of your actions when you drive. But in high-performance driving, the other guy is only part of the problem. On a lonely stretch of road the other guy isn't there, yet accidents continue to plague uncongested areas, and in the country, where impact speeds are generally more than 40 mph, the preponderance of fatal accidents occurs. You can "do yourself in" so easily that a part of your mind also has to be directed toward your car and yourself or the "other guy" won't even have to bother with you. The difference between city and country driving ought to be the difference between driving defensively and driving decisively.

Driving defensively you recognize that the biggest hazards are the cars around you—in front, on your sides, in the rear. You want to establish a buffer zone for yourself so that if anyone makes a mistake around you, you have room to maneuver. A clear road ahead and few, if any, cars around you can keep you out of accidents.

There are two ways to avoid the other guy. You can sit back and keep him in your sights, which means you still have to avoid him if he makes a mistake, or you can pass him and get out of his way. Given the choice, most drivers would rather create a situation than have to react to one created by someone else. If you know where you are, and where you're going, you're not at the total mercy of another's mistake.

What it amounts to is doing the other driver's thinking for him. Tricks like close lane changes, bursts of acceleration to pick up two car lengths, just put other drivers off. Give way to the other car even if you are clearly in the right. When you see that a truck or a car needs your space to merge, give it up gladly. If you have that buffer zone around you, there should always be room. Common-sense urban driving is signaling your intentions well in advance. It is also clearing the road if you suffer a breakdown.

You must recognize the consequences of your actions. For example, the entrance to a freeway is a decisive moment. You have, no doubt, run into that maddening coward who stops midway up a ramp, turns and looks over his shoulder to pick out a slot, then timidly pushes on. It is as dangerous as it is stupid. The time necessary to get up to speed is increased. If the ramp is clear it's much better to accelerate hard and make it very clear to those on the freeway that you mean to head for a particular spot and get there quickly, positively, and without delay. If you force a driver to apply his brakes when you join the fray, the driver behind him may overreact and so on down the line of traffic until far down the road the line of traffic will come to a stop, all because you didn't anticipate.

A great exercise is the "what if" game. Look at the car coming at you in the opposite lane and try to imagine what would happen if he came at you head on. Or, when a driver pulls out to pass you, think of your reaction if a car suddenly appeared and forced him back into your lane. The "what if" game builds anticipation. Visualize where each car around you would go if someone ran a red light. If you make a habit of this, you'll always have a plan worked out. You should not have to extemporize when you are behind the wheel.

This anticipation should extend to the ends of your field of vision. Visibility plays a vital role in driving, not only seeing but being seen. Any time you're behind another car or truck your field of vision is limited. The closer you are to the car in front, the more your vision suffers.

A surprising number of events take place even in the confines of a city that require the use of some of the elements discussed in this book. Knowing how to make the fullest and most efficient use of your brakes can save the front sheet metal time and time again. Knowing how to control a slide can keep you from smacking the curb as you dodge the poor soul who forgot to look coming out of his driveway. These and many other situations arise almost daily. If you know your limits and those of your car, chances are you'll keep that extra advantage on your side by holding the speed down when you share the public thoroughfares.

When you put the strictures of the city behind you, however, the essence of motoring comes to bloom. Things are in your hands then and controlling yourself with that burden bespeaks control. The point is that apex selection, weight shifts, lateral loadings, late-braking approaches, and maximum tire adhesion have little to do with motoring around a city, where just staying away from an accident about to happen takes up enough of the gray matter. Actually using the skills involved in high-performance driving should be brought to bear only when their use is justified. But you always want those skills close at hand in case they are needed. That means practice.

A trip over a mildly familiar road can be an interesting and enjoyable outing that can afford you a chance to stay in shape. Pick a road that will offer you the greatest challenge, not a superhighway. A mountain of some stature is usually at hand and can provide you with some educational moments. When you're touring the countryside, relaxed and alert in the grand style, your car working under you, there are few pleasures as personally satisfying.

It isn't necessary or even practical to try to make your absolute best time. You don't have to use all the road or totally vanquish it with raw speed to learn useful things about yourself and your car. On an open road you can practice double clutching, perfect your heel-and-toe procedures, and practice your ability to judge closing rates. All of these things can be performed without any regard to speed. Figuring out a corner before you get to it and employing a mini-line doesn't necessitate all-out tire slippage or an engine wound tight.

When you are moving along in your own lane minding your own business and tending to an appropriate speed you are exposed to little danger except when your path is crossed by access routes or by other drivers. It is a quiet time. When you are passing, or being passed, or when you're crossing a main road, you are exposed to danger. The time spent exposed to danger is what you want to reduce. You can't get rid of it completely but you can, by applying yourself, shorten the time when you are in the most danger. You do that with speed, not vehicle speed, but speed in your actions. If you are passing, get out past the guy and get it over with. Don't poke along, taking your own sweet time. Pull out, accelerate, and pull back in without disrupting the fellow you just passed.

Think far ahead of your location. Think your way around turns. Be ready to deal with any changes. If you are continually revising your estimation of what confronts you, the process will become automatic.

High-performance driving requires stamina but not the harsh physical kind. Holding your concentration is fatiguing and every trick you can employ to keep yourself alert should be used. Windows up, windows down. Tune the radio. Find a new station. Adjust your seat. Vary your speed. Keep your eyes moving. Do anything so you don't fall prey to road hypnosis. Shortening the "legs" of your tour will help.

If you can interpret those early signs of tension, move around in the seat, adjust the wheel, something that will give your muscles an adjustment. We all get stale when we sit too long in one position. Change your hand position on the wheel. When you make a pit stop, get out and stretch. A five-minute walk around a service island will refresh you.

Remember that pulling off the road for gas or a phone call breaks the rhythm you have established and it takes a while to get that concentration back.

Your eyes are the most critical fatigue area. Clean glasses and windshield can forestall many problems. Change your point of focus every few minutes. It is important that you don't look through the same spot in the windshield mile after mile. Alertness is directly tied to eye movement. Scientists are able to chart maximum mental activity in sleep just by monitoring small eye movements. When your eyes get heavy or surprises become too frequent, change your focus point. When it's bad, pull off. Driving when you are tired is not a good idea.

The time you select for your tour is no small consideration. Traveling during peak traffic hours or on weekends when many drivers who don't know the road are out is not recommended. By far the best time to motor at reasonable speed is in the small hours of the morning, long enough after the bars have closed so you don't have to deal with drunks. Also, at night you can see the headlights of an approaching car long before you actually meet it.

The freedom that comes with a deserted road has its disadvantages. If you go off the road, it may be some time before anyone finds you. You must also be aware that many odd machines are out at this time, farm vehicles and house-moving teams, to name but two.

Attempting to learn a road at night, however, is not a good idea. If it's a twisty road, you will encounter problems that have not been picked up by your headlights. It is very easy to overdrive your headlights when the road is clear. Try to avoid it. There is one benefit in nighttime travel over a strange road. You will be able to pick up the contour of the road quite easily. But this is moderated because you can't spot locating markers as easily in the darkness. Learn a road in the daylight hours. Practice at night.

When setting out to learn a road, pay close attention to the corners at the end of a straight. They can pull you in like a Venus flytrap. Marker posts, guardrails, warning signs, outcroppings of rock—all make good locators and they have a way of staying put, season after season. When you come across a particularly difficult corner make sure you have it located. First and foremost in your mind should be the braking distances into the more difficult bends.

You'll find that an hour of intense concentration takes a lot out of you. Just the process of identification is tiring. You get out of driving what you put into it. Don't overdo it the first time. It's nice to have something to go back to.

If you've set out in foul weather, you may be in for more than you bargained for. It just doesn't make sense to drive a car when conditions lend themselves to accidents. You may be confident but that won't help when a car looms up out of the fog sideways in your lane. Loss of visibility or traction should dictate a reduction in speed.

During the winter, shadows, shade, and valleys can keep the sun from melting the ice you think is gone. At night, the small patch of water that drained across the road can ice up readily. At 10 per cent tire efficiency, you're not going to be able to handle the situation. Rain isn't bad so long as the wipers are working and the ceiling hasn't dropped so low that you are in a cloud.

Country roads don't receive the maintenance of major arteries so you have to be on the lookout for debris. It occurs most often at the edges, of course, just where you want to place the wheels in following a line. The most exciting corner you have to negotiate may well be the one you create to avoid that old muffler. Expect a hazard around every bend.

High winds can be treacherous if you are on an exposed road. If you have been passed by that thundering semi coming the other way and have felt a blast of air push you over to the right, you understand air power. In open spaces, ride on the side of the lane nearest the wind so that any gust will center you in your lane instead of putting you over the center line and into possible danger. The wind factor has to be considered where the road runs in and out of obstructions such as buildings or tunnels or where it runs along the ridge line of a mountain. It is the surprise of the gust that gets you.

Any car pushing its way through the air at 60 mph is encountering no small force. The air packs up around the front of the car and flows back over it in a turbulent manner to the rear where an area of relatively stable air follows in the car's wake. Actually, this is a low-pressure area. As the speed of the car increases, this area of low pressure lengthens. When the speed hits 100 mph, this low-pressure area that trails the car can be used for slipstreaming, or drafting. Slipstreaming is for race tracks only. First, you have to be going so fast to get any benefit from it. Second, following that close you have to have complete trust in the driver ahead. Third, riding the lead car's bumper any place but a racetrack, where everyone knows what comes next, means you have only a fraction of a second to react. As an individual, your concern should be used for contemplating the air packed up in front of your car, rather than what's trailing.

Wind resistance, when added to rolling resistance, can be used to save the brakes when it's time to slow from a rapid rate. The air mass that a car pushes through begins to have real power at 60 miles an hour and up. When you pass the century mark it can be a difficult problem. A car with plenty of power but a poorly designed shape will never hit its top speed as the effects of the air running over and under it take weight from the tires. Worse than the loss of absolute speed is the loss in directional control. High speeds can make a car very antsy. High speeds in high winds are to be avoided.

One of the worst moments on a tour can come when the weather decides to change. During the first few minutes of rain, take extra care. The oil and rubber deposits laid down by other cars are lifted from the tiny cracks and crevices of the road and neither of them mix well with water so they form a film on top. The moisture under the oil and rubber makes for a very slippery surface. The two worst moments I've ever encountered came during this condition.

Roads, by their nature, make excellent drainage channels. Tire treads are designed to wipe away up to three-quarters of an inch of water, something you might experience in a heavy downpour, but larger accumulations can cause tricky moments. The danger comes when the tires start acting like boats and get up on top of the water in what is called "hydroplaning." When the speed is great, the tire, as it rolls over the water, pushes a bow wave of water ahead of it, and when the speed is great enough or the water is deep enough, this bow wave has no place to go and so it curls under the tire, lifting the tire from the roadway and putting it on top of the water. The tire has actually broken contact with the road and you can expect the same kind of control in that situation as when you are in the air.

Railroad tracks also cause some scary hassles. Railroad tracks, if they parallel your lane, can be a deadly enemy if one or more tires finds its way into the channel. The tire then wants to follow the track. In the wet, the problem is magnified. Wet steel has poor friction characteristics and hitting the brakes or trying to turn may produce no effect at all. Railroad crossings also have a way of getting you airborne. Roads and railroads just don't mix.

Part of what makes an above-average driver is his confidence. Confidence is something gained only with experience. When you see that you have controlled a situation, you're not likely to be frightened of it again. The finest confidence builder is that skid pad. Using it will let you know exactly what your car will do and how well you can control it. That experience will keep you from getting in over your head. Confidence leads to decisive action. There is one mistake you don't want to make in a car. It is the sin of doing nothing. Freezing up, or giving yourself to fate, is as unnatural as it is foolish. Even if you find you're going to crash, that last attempt at control can mean the difference between a stiff neck and a broken one. You cannot quit on a car.

Remember, too, there are lessons in errors. Reviewing your performance, even if it ended with your being off the road, is something that should come at the end of every tour.

And finally, check your car thoroughly, use all the safety measures available to you, run within your capabilities, and you will have more enjoyment from your machine than you ever thought possible.

13
THE BEST START

On any Sunday throughout America, many automotive events take place. These events may be anything from a slalom laid out in a parking lot to a legal-speed rally run through city streets. Or it might be a club event of a hodgepodge of cars driven by men who have no desire to get out with the "big boys" but still enjoy competitive motoring with like-minded friends.

This substrata of racing seldom receives the attention it deserves. It serves as social club and outlet for thousands of dyed-in-the-wool enthusiasts.

Automotive buffs tend to stick together by banding up to form car clubs for distinct marques. MG owners get to know other MG owners, Datsun drivers pal around with other Datsun drivers, and so on. If you already have a sports car or a sports sedan, chances are you'll find a club in your area. A little investigation can lead you to them. Start at the local dealership. Car buffs tend to have stronger ties with dealers and mechanics than do average owners. Listings of car club events are sometimes posted in the paper, particularly the Sunday sports section.

All you need is the car and one contact and you have it made. The love for a car can be addictive and getting together with other addicts makes the affliction easier to bear. Most, if not all, of these clubs are open to men and women. The wife or girl friend will be far more understanding if you ask her to come along. A car club is as viable a social outlet as a bridge game and perhaps more fun. Women can drive as well as men and are just as capable of learning how to control a car at speed. Some events, by the way, are overnight affairs, and everybody needs a navigator.

In finding a club you are on your way to new knowledge about your car and your abilities. Friendships among members are worthwhile and the information you can pick up is endless—what tires seem to be best for your car, what modifications can be done for little money to improve handling, where the funky roads are, and in what areas car trouble appears most often.

Subscriptions to some of the magazines dedicated to automobiles can guide you to your brethren, too. In most of these magazines you'll find listings for various clubs throughout the country. *Car and Driver* and *Road & Track* are but two of the premier monthlies in the field. Look for *Competition Press and AUTOWEEK,* a weekly newspaper that is filled with information about what happened last week and what's on tap for the next.

A wealth of information and enjoyment can be found in these publications, and it doesn't cost much to get your feet wet. By reading, you'll keep up with automobiles as they develop. In these days of emission controls, federal regulations, and the industry's full-out attempt to produce cars that conform to new standards, cars are changing radically. New terminology and new techniques will develop to go along with these newer cars, and if you're not keeping up, you're falling behind.

Another excellent avenue for the enthusiast is going to the races. The things you've learned in this book can be seen on the tracks now that you know what the drivers are trying to do. Any kind of racing is worth the journey.

There is as much exciting action on half-mile tracks as there is in off-road races, although the latter events can be tough on spectators. You probably know about the major tracks, whether for stockers or Grand Prix machines. But there may be several other tracks in your area where nonsanctioned events take place. Automobile racing is second only to horse racing as a spectator sport and that means there is a good chance something is going on all around you.

The real fun comes, however, when you are a competitor, not a spectator. There are hundreds of small events that don't require a competition license, and you need only a car, any car, in good condition in order to compete. But look before you leap. Plan a tour to a small event and watch the proceedings. If you have any competitive fire, one outing should have you coming back for more. It's so easy to say, "I can do as well as those guys." The proof is on the track.

If you see yourself getting into club racing, you'll want to make sure your car is in excellent shape. There is a technical inspection before most events and officials check for the proper seat belts, assign you a class, and make sure you have a good set of brakes. It's no fun to drive to an event and be told you can't go out on the track.

Small slaloms or gymkhanas are fun and fairly safe. Fairly safe should be underlined because like anything else there are levels. An older, more established club may put on a real speed show. Most, however, are twisty low-gear courses. In the beginning, it's not so much a question of winning as it is of gaining your confidence. If you're good, it will show up in the times.

If you have discovered that driving at speed is your "bag" but the car you own is unsatisfactory, you're probably thinking or dreaming of another car. Join the crowd. There are so many fine machines available that the selection is dazzling. The pocketbook seems to be the only limiting factor. Don't overreach on a car. It's no fun to be tied down and it's even less fun if you can't give a car the attention it deserves. Always consider the maintenance. When you drive a car near its limits, it is tough on engine, brakes, and tires. They are all expensive items to replace.

Make a list of your requirements in a car: the number of people you usually transport, the roads you drive on, the number of miles you will put on it. It is pretty easy, considering the possibilities, to fit a car to your wallet and requirements if you know what both are.

Don't agonize because you can't do with a two-seater. There are several four- and five-passenger sedans that are not only fun to drive but are practical as well.

If you are looking into used cars expect to be aggravated. Some previous owners have had no regard for their car while others may have lavished such care on their baby that you can't tell it from a new one. Selection is as varied as people. Buying a used sports car or sports sedan is not something to be rushed into. Take your time and look for the best.

All of us would like to have a long-legged car with superior handling and power but the truth must be faced in this day of growing regulations and restrictions. You just cannot use all of a car on American roads and knowing that should affect your choice of your next car. There's no sense owning a car you can't use.

If you accept the hypothesis that the driving, not the car, is the way to judge a man, and that it would be more fun for the driver to use all of his car rather than 80 per cent of its potential, then you won't have as much trouble finding a car that suits your needs.

Wringing the last ounce of performance out of a car with a willing engine and a sophisticated suspension is a lot more fun for the driver. An underpowered car keeps you busy and can provide just as much satisfaction as another, more powerful car. In fact, it's probably more satisfying to do more with less. The satisfaction becomes very personal. It's just harder on the ego.

A car used as a status symbol is nothing new. A car, make no mistake, is a wonderful ego extension. But what level do you want? Do you want to show off the size of your treasury or demonstrate your knowledge of cars? Do you want to be the keeper of a super car or the driver of a distinctive car? Do you want to lay back and let the car take the glory or make your abilities as a driver the yardstick?

Almost anyone can deal with gobs of power and get around quickly but only the few can get the most out of their brakes, transmission, tires, and suspension. A car that can stop with authority, is capable of taking severe evasive action in stride, and can still keep up with traffic is perhaps your best bet. Put your money in the total car. It's great sport to beat a car that costs more and has more power. When you do that, you win, not the car.

Exhilaration and satisfaction await the driver who consistently demonstrates his mastery over not only the car but himself as well. There is nothing to compare with the thrills a car can provide for the man who loves life when it's lived on the edge.

High-performance driving is an art, an art that must be experienced to be appreciated. Hopefully, what you've read will build your skills past mere proficiency and on to the next level, appreciation. When you respect and appreciate an automobile, consistency and control flow from the driver to the machine, the proper path. Like so many other things, the danger comes when the thing possesses you, instead of the other way around.

Good luck and safe motoring.

APPENDIX
WHERE TO START

If you are thinking about racing you have to face certain questions and facts that will have a direct bearing on your decision. There are really only two questions though each has many variations.

First, are you prepared to risk your life? To be sure, there is a risk just getting out of bed or crossing the street; but if you race, you will be deliberately placing your life in jeopardy. A man isn't always killed at the wheel but often suffers cruel and debilitating injuries that can leave him crippled or a vegetable for life. A future like that makes for despair, remorse, and places a heavy burden on your family. Ernest Hemingway said that there were only three sports as far as he was concerned—motor racing, bullfighting, and mountain climbing. In each, a man deliberately puts his life on the line, perhaps to find meaning through risk.

You have to have complete trust in yourself. A mistake in any of the three sports can kill you. It is, beyond all else, a personal decision, one that must take into account those liabilities and responsibilities you have taken on yourself. Wife, children, family, and friends are just a few of these.

Secondly, consider the money involved. An SCCA club racer in one of the minor classes (those not so hotly contested) will certainly spend $5,000 a year and probably much more. And that doesn't include the original cost of the equipment! Car maintenance costs money. Even more, it takes time—time preparing the car, time getting to the race course, and time repairing what you are sure to break. And time spent on your car is time taken from somewhere else. There is much excitement and enjoyment at smaller rallies, slaloms, and gymkhanas.

The risks, of course, are decreased in proportion to the speed. On this level you can spend whatever you have in mind, from $200 on up.

If you still have the bug and a car that seems to be begging for a race, get in touch with the Sports Car Club of America, Post Office Box 22476, Denver, Colorado 80222. Tell them what you have in mind.

The SCCA controls most of the racing in this country and the staff's expertise can help smooth out your path. They run excellent training programs all over the country and if you have the car, properly prepared, they'll get you started. Dues are $25 a year.

It may be that you don't own or have access to a competition car but still want to see if you have what it takes to race. In this case, don't despair. If you have the time and the money—one week and from $500 to $800, there are quite a few professional driving schools that have top-notch instructors and excellent race cars for your use. They are located in the North, South, East, and West.

The price if you use the school cars is higher. Even if you own your car, you might consider the benefits of using another car while you learn. Mistakes are common in the beginning.

One item about professional schools should be mentioned. You are not there for a vacation. You are there to learn, so you have to bring the proper attitude with you and be prepared to soak up information, which means concentration. If they see you aren't sincere you'll be black flagged before you start. What you learn can get you off to a good beginning toward that competition license and, moreover, can save your life countless times on today's roads.

In the West, near Los Angeles, there are two schools. The Bob Bondurant School of High-Performance Driving uses the Sears Point Raceway. Write to him there at Highways 37 and 121, Sonoma, California 95476. If you use the school cars the tab is $800 and one week of your time.

Also close to Los Angeles, and using the Willow Springs Raceway, is the Jim Russell Racing Drivers School, Post Office Box 911, Rosamond, California 93560. The cost for the Russell school runs $500 for the entire course.

Considering the equipment you drive and the end result, it's worth twice the price to attend these schools. They operate all year round.

In the East we have the eastern branch of the Jim Russell School, 723 Halpern Avenue, Dorval 760, P.Q., Quebec, which operates out of Le Circuit Mont Tremblant, north of Montreal. Here the course is $500 and takes three days. It is a bargain because the Russell school has some attractive benefits, such as a chance to race professionally and win a trip to England.

Also in the East, there is the Bill Scott Racing School, 1420 Springhill Road, McLean, Virginia 22101. The schooling process is broken into two divisions, two days each, and the car is supplied. The first session, for beginners, is $215, and the second session is $375. Because it is located near Washington, D.C., the Scott school draws from the southern section of the states.

Fred Opert Racing School, 17 Industrial Avenue, Upper Saddle River, New Jersey 07458, has fine cars, professional instructors, and uses the Bridgehampton Race Circuit, 100 miles or so from New York City. For $500 and three days you get the whole treatment. Remember that these eastern schools have to contend with weather and are open from May to October.

If you can't go east or west, you may go north. A school that has quite a program is located in Michigan. The Road Sports International Racing Drivers School, 2241 West Liberty, Ann Arbor, Michigan 48103, has what appears to be some excellent programs for beginners and experts alike. The cost should run just over $500 for the whole shebang.

These schools will be happy to send out more information to those of you who are seriously considering racing. You should be in reasonably good health, over twenty-one (though you can sign up at sixteen in some and eighteen in all if you have a parental waiver), and they'll fill you in on the particulars when you contact them.

These professional schools are recognized by the SCCA, and by completing the courses to the satisfaction of the instructors, you can cut 50 per cent of the SCCA requirements from your competition license. You will still have to go through part of the SCCA's school program.

These schools are heartily recommended. They provide the perfect environment for you to learn about yourself and your abilities. The on-site guidance is important when you set out to learn the concepts involved in high-performance driving.